FULL-STACK iOS
DEVELOPMENT
WITH SWIFT AND VAPOR

FULL-STACK iOS
DEVELOPMENT
WITH SWIFT AND VAPOR

Hem Dutt

MERCURY LEARNING AND INFORMATION
Boston, Massachusetts

Publisher: David Pallai
MERCURY LEARNING AND INFORMATION
121 High Street, 3rd Floor
Boston, MA 02110
info@merclearning.com
www.merclearning.com
800-232-0223

H. Dutt. *Full-Stack iOS Development with Swift and Vapor.*
ISBN: 978-1-50152-257-4

Library of Congress Control Number: 2024939127

242526321   This book is printed on acid-free paper in the United States of America.

Our titles are available for adoption, license, or bulk purchase by institutions, corporations, etc. For additional information, please contact the Customer Service Dept. at 800-232-0223 (toll free).

All of our titles are available in digital format at academiccourseware.com and other digital vendors. *Companion files (code samples and figures) are available for downloading (with proof of purchase) by writing to the publisher at info@merclearning.com.* The sole obligation of MERCURY LEARNING AND INFORMATION to the purchaser is to replace the files, based on defective materials or faulty workmanship, but not based on the operation or functionality of the product.

This book is dedicated to students and software engineers embarking on their journey as full-stack developers or exploring the dynamic iOS domain. May it inspire and empower you to unlock your full potential in this exciting field. Together, let us embrace the world of full-stack iOS development and strive for excellence.

CONTENTS

Preface   *xiii*

Acknowledgments   *xvii*

About the Author   *xix*

Chapter 1: Full-Stack Development Overview   **1**

   Introduction   1

   Structure   1

   Introduction to Full-Stack Development   2

   Brief History   4

      Full-Stack: What Does It Mean?   5

   Minimum Viable Product (MVP)   5

      Airbnb   6

      Foursquare   6

   Problems with Full-Stack Development   7

   Advantages of Full-Stack Development   10

   Swift on Server and Vapor   11

   Swift Packages for Back-End Development   14

      SwiftNIO   14

      AsyncHTTPClient   15

      Swift AWS Lambda Runtime   16

Soto—AWS SDK Swift 16

Conclusion 17

Chapter 2: Setting Up the Environment **19**

Introduction 19

Structure 19

Installation of Xcode 20

Installation of the Vapor Toolbox 21

Hello World Project (Vapor) 22

    Build and Run Project 22

    Folder Structure 24

        Public Folder 25

        Sources 25

        Run 25

        Tests 26

Swift Package Manager 26

Hello World Project (iOS) 27

    Project Structure 31

        Add Hello World Label 32

Run Xcode Project 35

Conclusion 39

Chapter 3: Routing, MVC, and JSON in Vapor **41**

Introduction 41

Structure 41

Objectives 42

Routes 42

Router Methods 43

    Basic Routes 43

    Nested Routes 44

    Route Parameters 47

    Anything Routes and Catch-All Routes 50

    Query Strings 52

    Route Groups 53

Model-View-Controller (MVC) 55

Working with JSON 63

    Posting JSON and Postman App 67

Conclusion 73

Chapter 4: Async and HTML Rendering in Vapor **75**

Introduction 75

Structure 75

Objectives 75

Async 76

    Async Await 76

    Migrating to Async/Await 76

Logging 77

Environment 79

Errors 80

    Abort 80

        Abort Error 81

        Debuggable Error 83

Stack Traces 85

    Swift Backtrace 85

        Error Traces 85

        ErrorMiddleware 86

Leaf 87

Conclusion 94

Chapter 5: PostgreSQL Integration in Vapor **95**

Introduction 95

Structure 95

Objectives 96

Data Persistence with Vapor 96

Installing and Setting Up PostgreSQL 96

Fluent ORM 104

    Adding Fluent to a New Project 104

    Adding Fluent to an Existing Project 107

CRUD Operations   107

Migrations   110

Postico   112

Create and Save Model   116

    Create Model   116

    Save Model   116

Conclusion   121

Chapter 6: Building User Interfaces for iOS   **123**

Introduction   123

Structure   123

Auto Layout with Storyboards   124

Swift UI   135

    Working with Text   137

    Working with Images   140

    Working with Stacks   144

Conclusion   148

Chapter 7: Data Persistence with Core Data and SQLite in iOS   **149**

Introduction   149

Structure   149

Core Data   150

    Core Data Stack   150

    Include Core Data in a New Project   151

    Include Core Data in an Existing Project   152

    CRUD Operations   154

        Codegen   158

        Category/Extension   159

    Core Data Migrations   161

Lightweight Data Migration   162

Networking   164

Protocol Support   165

Conclusion   165

Chapter 8: Full-Stack Implementation   **167**

Introduction   167

Structure   167

Objectives   168

Project Outline   168

Setup Remote Database   168

Server App   171

     Models   172

     Migrations   175

     Controllers   177

     Config and Routes   180

iOS App   184

     Models   185

Networking   187

User Interface   192

Test Run   201

Conclusion   203

Chapter 9: Advanced Full-Stack Concepts   **205**

Introduction   205

Structure   205

Objectives   205

Middleware   206

     Creating Middleware   207

WebSockets   209

     Messages   209

         Sending   210

         Receiving   210

         Closing   211

APNS   211

Security   216

     Authentication   216

Basic Authentication   217

Bearer Authentication   219

Composition   220

Session   222

JWT   224

KeyChain   226

Adding a Password to Keychain   227

Conclusion   229

Chapter 10: Deploying iOS and Vapor Applications   231

Introduction   231

Structure   231

Objectives   232

Vapor App Deployment   232

Heroku   232

Docker   236

Set up Docker   237

Build and Run   239

Production Deployment   239

iOS App Deployment   240

Code Signing   240

Create App Store Connect Record for the App   241

Add New App   242

Archive and Upload the App   242

Configure the App's Metadata in App Store Connect   244

Submit App for Review   245

Conclusion   247

Index   249

PREFACE

In this book, we explore the combined power of the Swift programming language, the Vapor framework, and iOS development in order to master the realm of full-stack iOS development.

In today's interconnected world, the demand for versatile developers who can seamlessly bridge the gap between the backend and frontend is skyrocketing. As the boundaries between server-side and client-side become increasingly blurred, mastering full-stack development has become a valuable skill set.

This book is designed to cater to a wide range of readers, from aspiring developers and students to seasoned iOS professionals seeking to expand their expertise. Whether you are taking your first steps in Swift or are already well-versed in the language, this book equips you with the knowledge and tools necessary to navigate the world of full-stack iOS development with confidence.

We begin by laying the foundation, exploring the essentials of Vapor, Swift, and iOS app development. From there, we cover backend development, covering topics such as persisting data, working with models, and integrating APIs. Simultaneously, we discuss front-end development, unraveling the intricacies of creating compelling user interfaces, networking, and authentication.

Throughout this journey, we emphasize best practices, security considerations, and performance optimization techniques to ensure that you not only build functional applications but also create robust, secure, and high-performing ones.

Real-world projects and hands-on exercises will guide you, allowing you to apply your newly acquired knowledge to practical scenarios. You will witness the power of integrating Swift and Vapor, leveraging their synergistic potential to develop innovative full-stack iOS applications.

I invite you to embark on this transformative journey of becoming a full-stack iOS developer:

Chapter 1: Full-Stack Development Overview – This chapter aims to give a basic understanding of the term "full-stack development," a brief history of its emergence, and the concept of a minimum viable product. We will also explore the problems and advantages associated with full-stack development and provide a brief introduction to Swift on the server.

Chapter 2: Setting Up the Environment – This chapter aims to provide a basic understanding of the tools and SDKs necessary to begin with Vapor and iOS development. In this chapter, we will cover the installation processes for Xcode, Vapor Toolbox, and starter projects in Vapor, as well as for iOS.

Chapter 3: Routing, MVC, and JSON in Vapor – This chapter aims to provide a basic understanding of the process of creating routes for the server application, a brief understanding of the MVC design pattern, and the creation of controllers in a Vapor application. Furthermore, we will explore the JSON format and handling JSON in a Vapor app and extend this discussion. We will also cover the Postman app that can be used for testing the routes.

Chapter 4: Async and HTML Rendering in Vapor – This chapter aims to extend the basic understanding of Async, Logging, Capturing, Stack Traces, and finally, handling HTML rendering in a Vapor project. In this chapter, we will implement a small part of the code to highlight HTML rendering on a Web page using Leaf and Vapor routes.

Chapter 5: PostgreSQL Integration in Vapor – In this chapter, we will study the integration of PostgreSQL with Vapor. PostgreSQL is an open-source, relational database system that focuses on extensibility and standards. It is designed for enterprise use and also has native support for geometric primitives such as coordinates, which come in handy when working with Fluent. It also supports these primitives and saves nested types, such as dictionaries, directly into PostgreSQL.

Chapter 6: Building User Interfaces for iOS – The aim of this chapter is to further the understanding of the basic building blocks of iOS UI development and complete the circle of full-stack development with Swift.

Chapter 7: Data Persistence with Core Data and SQLite in iOS – Implement data persistence on iOS using Core Data with SQLite as a persistent store. In this chapter, we will write our very first Core Data implementation for storing data in an iOS app. By the end of this chapter, readers will be able to: model data using Xcode's model editor; add new records to Core Data; fetch a set of records from Core Data; display the fetched records; and learn the basics of Networking.

Chapter 8: Full-Stack Implementation – We implemented small sample codes to facilitate understanding of Vapor and iOS app development. These samples were discussed in isolation to enable readers to grab specific concepts without worrying about the larger picture. In this chapter, we will specifically look into the larger picture and the full-stack implementation of an app.

Chapter 9: Advanced Full-Stack Concepts – In this chapter, we will explore some advanced topics related to full-stack development, which are especially important with respect to overall system design and architecture. Mastering these concepts is essential for commercial application development.

Chapter 10: Deploying iOS and Vapor Applications – The objective of this chapter is to thoroughly examine the deployment process(es) for both our iOS and Vapor apps, making them accessible to the public. For Vapor apps, we will explore deployment via Heroku and Docker. Meanwhile, for iOS apps, the App Store serves as the sole avenue for deployment, and we will cover that process as well in this chapter.

Companion Files: Code samples and figures from the text are available for downloading by writing to the publisher at info@merclearning.com.

By the end of this book, you will have the knowledge and confidence to leverage the combined power of the Swift programming language, the Vapor framework, and iOS development in order to master the realm of full-stack iOS development.

ACKNOWLEDGMENTS

I have to start by thanking my beloved wife, Payal Bhardwaj, for keeping me motivated throughout my journey as a writer. She is always by my side and supports me in fulfilling my dreams, however impossible they seem to others. Thank you a ton, my dear, for being the pillar of my strength. You are a superwoman.

I must offer special thanks to my parents, who nurtured my childhood and, despite their limited means, provided me with the best they could do and shaped my character.

I would also like to thank the technical reviewers and editors for helping me shape the chapters and content of this book.

I would also like to thank my colleagues and friends, who have always believed in me and encouraged me.

Finally, and most importantly, I would like to acknowledge my two beautiful children, Adwit and Anika. Thanks, Adwit, for being such a sweetheart and adorable baby and filling the environment with unconditional love, and Anika, for being such a powerhouse and my super girl! I love you both so much.

ABOUT THE AUTHOR

Hem Dutt began his software engineering career in 2010 as a macOS (OS X) and iOS application developer and thereafter designed and developed numerous native macOS and iOS applications for various clients across the globe, while working for multiple MNCs. With more than a decade of experience working on macOS and iOS, Hem Dutt has developed and managed applications in multiple domains, including healthcare, insurance, VPN clients, publishing, IOT, and VoIP. His passion for designing and developing secure, reliable, and modular software is evident from his blogs, client awards and recommendations, and open-source projects. Prior to this book, he authored "Interprocess Communication with macOS: Apple IPC Methods," cementing his expertise in the Apple ecosystem.

CHAPTER

1

FULL-STACK DEVELOPMENT OVERVIEW

INTRODUCTION

This chapter aims to provide readers with a basic understanding of the term *full-stack development*, tracing a brief history of the term and that of the minimum viable product concept. We will also explore the problems and advantages of full-stack development and provide a brief introduction to Swift on the server.

STRUCTURE

In this chapter, we will cover the following topics:

- Introduction to full-stack development
- Brief history
- Minimum viable product (MVP)
- Problems with full-stack development
- Advantages of full-stack development
- Swift on server and Vapor
- Swift packages for back-end development

INTRODUCTION TO FULL-STACK DEVELOPMENT

The term "full-stack developer" is commonly used in the software industry, typically referring to a Web developer who can build the front-end and back-end of a Web app. Instead of specializing, a full-stack developer is able to work across the back-end and front-end spectrums of app development.

It is an already established fact that being a specialist in one field or technology and gaining mastery in that particular aspect of technology has distinct advantages, but in the modern world, as technology is rapidly changing and evolving, many companies are seeking talented developers who are able to understand and work on the entire spectrum of front- and back-end technologies and are able to create a usable end product. The survey provided by HackerRank on the most sought-after talent pool in 2020 provides a good insight into the demand for full-stack developers.

As per the HackerRank report, across company sizes, hiring managers agree that full-stack developers are a top priority. According to 38% of hiring managers, it is the #1 role to fill in 2020. Back-end developers and data scientists were ranked second and third priorities, respectively.

Emphasis on full-stack developers was most pronounced in small companies (1–49 employees), 43% of which ranked the role as their top priority.

Though the qualities that define a *full-stack developer* are a subject of debate, most agree that they should have a basic understanding (or better) of all layers of a tech stack and should be able to generate a minimum viable product on their own. This is why they are especially important in small organizations, where fewer employees often have to do the job of many. See the following figure.

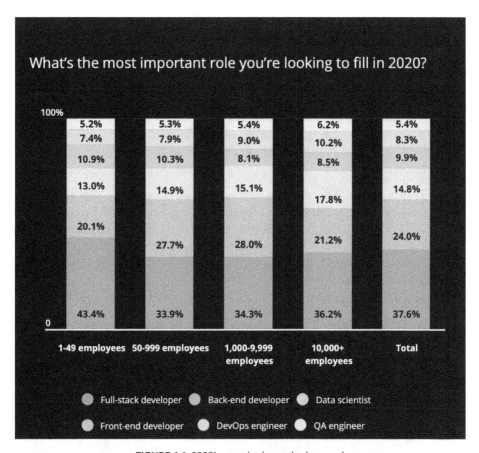

FIGURE 1.1 2020's most in-demand talent pool.
(source: https://info.hackerrank.com/rs/487-WAY-049/images/HackerRank-2020-Developer-Skills-Report.pdf)

As is clear from the report, these developers, also known as *full-stack developers*, are *once again* in demand. Does this mean this is not a new phenomenon? Yes, this role has a long history and has had its share of ups and downs, as well as arguments and disagreements from all kinds of people about what a full-stack developer really means and what the level of expertise of the developer in different aspects of the stack should be.

Full-stack developers are useful as generalists who can quickly come up with a **minimum viable product** (**MVP**) on their own. They can also be very helpful in providing insight into the entire application infrastructure and contributing to all its parts. It is a sought-after ability for many roles in the software development industry.

BRIEF HISTORY

If we take a broader view, full-stack development has been integral to the programming world since the very beginning, but it was not understood in its current context before.

Full-stack development in the public domain only came to light in 2008, when designing for the Web as well as mobile became mainstream. Earlier, this term was used with varying understandings regularly in the 1970s as well as the 1980s.

The main reason for this was that, at that time, there was not much difference between a back-end programmer and a front-end programmer. Slowly, with time, the distinction between front-end and back-end became defined, and two different streams of application development came into existence, namely, front-end and back-end development. In 2008, the concept of full-stack Web development gained momentum, and with passing years, it has become one of the most in-demand job roles of the present time.

According to the 2021 developer survey by Stack Overflow, over 49.47% of developers describe themselves as full-stack developers. See the following figure.

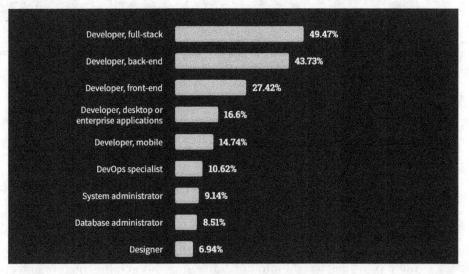

FIGURE 1.2 Developer roles.
(source: https://insights.stackoverflow.com/survey/2021#developer-profile-developer-roles)

During all these times, the term *full-stack* has gained traction in the Web developer community, but an obvious question is whether it can be applied to mobile application development. This is an interesting question: What constitutes a full-stack mobile app developer?

As we know, mobile app developers work on the client side of applications, or, in loose terms, front-end, and therefore, it might seem logical to assume that a mobile app developer simply needs the skill to develop a back-end to be a full-stack developer.

However, this is not as simple as it looks, and we are going to explore why it is a lot more complicated in the context of an iOS developer.

Full-Stack: What Does It Mean?

The term "stack" here refers to the collection of technologies needed to build an application. For example:

LAMP (Linux, Apache, MySQL, and PHP) or **MEAN (MongoDB, Express, Angular, and NodeJS)** or **MERN (MongoDB, Express, ReactJS, and NodeJS)**, and so on are technology stacks that have all the parts needed to build a minimum viable product of a Web app.

To understand the term "full-stack" in terms of iOS development, let us use the MERN preceding example and substitute React with Swift to replace the front-end part in a Web app stack with native Swift. Therefore, a full-stack on iOS might resemble **MESN** (MongoDB, Express, Swift, and NodeJS).

MINIMUM VIABLE PRODUCT (MVP)

As discussed in previous sections, full-stack developers are useful as generalists who can quickly come up with a **minimum viable product** (**MVP**) on their own. Let us understand what an MVP is.

A minimum viable product, or MVP, is a product with only enough features to onboard initial targeted customers and validate a product-market fit for a business idea early in the product development cycle. In the software industry, the MVP can actually help the product team receive early user feedback and make it possible to iterate and improve the product.

The basic idea of agile methodology is built on a process for validating and iterating products based on short user input cycles, and so the MVP plays a central role in agile development.

MVP can be understood as the initial version of a new product that allows a team to get the maximum feedback and customer validation from customers with the least amount of effort.

A company might decide to develop and release a minimum viable product because of the following:

- The company wants to release the product to the market as quickly as possible with basic features to gain an early-mover advantage.

- The company wants to test the idea with real target customers before committing a large budget to the product's full development.

MVP has the following two distinct features:

- It has enough features for consumers to purchase the product.

- It has a feedback mechanism for users so that the company can collect real data for product-market fit.

If you are still wondering what this would look like in the real world, let us examine the stories of a couple of brands that launched successful MVPs.

Airbnb

With limited funds to build the business, the founders used their own apartments to validate their idea of creating a market offering peer-to-peer rental housing online. They created a minimalist Web site, conducted marketing campaigns about their property, and found several customers almost immediately.

Foursquare

The location-based social network Foursquare started with just a one-feature MVP, that is, offering only check-ins and gamification rewards. The development and production teams of Foursquare then added recommendations, city guides, and other features until they validated the idea with an ever-growing user base.

PROBLEMS WITH FULL-STACK DEVELOPMENT

One of the problems with the term *full-stack* is that it does not exactly define the skill level needed by the developer across the stack. For example, how can we gauge the threshold skill needed from a full-stack iOS developer to develop a Web site at a bare minimum? A full-stack iOS developer should know how to put together a simple static Web site using HTML and CSS, for example, to play a YouTube video URL within the app.

However, if the developer is working on a complex social networking app, that will require an admin portal to control users' permissions based on various parameters and will also require a lot of other complex user flows such as authentication, data storage, and APIs.

Both of these scenarios will require a huge shift in terms of the expertise needed in various stacks. Generally speaking, the expectation from a *full-stack* iOS developer is to have deep expertise in the iOS domain and basic knowledge of how to put together simple Web apps using HTML and CSS.

At the other end of iOS app development, there are hybrid app developers who use frameworks such as React Native and Flutter to develop Web and mobile apps. It seems much easier to earn the title "full-stack" going the hybrid way, but native iOS app development has its own merits, and hybrid and native app developers are generally not the same.

We also need to understand that, in practice, a full-stack iOS developer might not complete a real project on his or her own. Although theoretically possible, an individual developing all parts of a project implies a lot of risks. In practice, a full-stack iOS developer is a generalist who has a deep understanding of one or two components of the full-stack and a high level of knowledge of the rest. This makes a full-stack iOS developer suitable for creating minimum viable projects, proof of concepts, and leading an overall project at a high level.

The fact that there is no well-defined and concrete definition of a full-stack developer and that the role requires continuous juggling of technologies is validated by the survey for 2020 from HackerRank. As per the survey, full-stack developers are required to learn new skills most often.

As per the HackerRank report, full-stack developers may be in the highest demand, but their role is also one of the most professionally demanding. Sixty percent of full-stack developers were required to learn a completely new framework or platform in the last year—more than any other role polled.

Full-stack developers also have to learn the most languages: 45% reported that they had to pick up a new one within the last year. Their peers have to learn more about theoretical concepts; data scientists and DevOps engineers were required to learn new concepts most often (33%).

With expertise that spans front-end, back-end, and more (depending on whom you ask), full-stack developers have one of the more nebulous job descriptions in the technical world. The relative flexibility of their role—and the breadth of technologies they have to keep up with as a result—means learning on the job never stops. See the following figure.

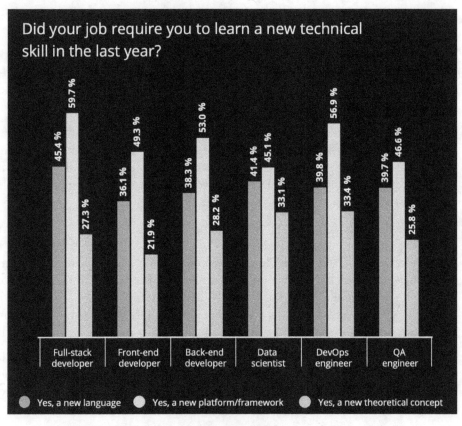

FIGURE 1.3 Full-stack developers are required to learn new skills most often. *(source: https://info.hackerrank.com/rs/487-WAY-049/images/HackerRank-2020-Developer-Skills-Report.pdf)*

As is evident from the data, full-stack development is gaining traction, but it has its own unique problems, even more aggravated in the case of full-stack mobile development. Therefore, as it always happens in such cases, the industry is divided on this subject.

People on the anti-full-stack developer side argue for what does or does not constitute full-stack development. The anti-full-stack argument is centered on the idea that a full-stack developer should have the ability to easily navigate between back-end and front-end development with a high level of expertise.

The anti-full-stack argument says that to be really effective, full-stack developers should be able to:

- Write high-quality code for the client side, which should be on par with a senior client-side developer.

- Write equally high-quality code for the server side, which should be on par with a senior server-side developer.

- Manage the infrastructure and deployment on the server side.

- Manage client application releases (on the App Store in the case of the iOS app).

While many developers can do some work that covers both disciplines, very few can do both well.

Therefore, against full-stack development, the argument is that a truly full-stack developer is almost impossible to find, and while too many people boast of themselves as full-stack developers, they do not have full-stack qualifications in reality.

In a way, it seems that it is an unrealistic demand. A true full-stack developer should have *dual mastery* of both the client and server sides, which is almost impossible given the speed at which new technology is evolving. The argument against full-stack developers is that this encourages wide breadth and shallow-depth knowledge and does not allow an individual to attain expertise.

ADVANTAGES OF FULL-STACK DEVELOPMENT

As discussed in the previous section, there are visible problems in understanding full-stack development and what the expectation should be from a full-stack developer. For practical purposes, we can understand full-stack development with a broader interpretation of the term. The idea that a full-stack developer has to be an expert in every layer of the tech stack is an unreasonable expectation, and instead, if they have working knowledge of the entire stack with expertise in only a few layers, this should be good enough for all practical implications.

We can see the definition of *full-stack* development for a less strict set of requirements, described as follows:

- Comfortable with writing both client-side and back-end code with moderate expertise in one and deep expertise in another.

- Can generate a minimum viable product (MVP) with minimal support from others.

- Provide expert-level specialty on either the client or server side.

- Have at least a high-level understanding of technologies throughout the stack.

If we follow this definition, a full-stack developer does not have to be an expert in every layer of the tech stack. Instead, here, "full-stack developer" means someone who is an effective and seasoned generalist who has a wide knowledge base, a deep specialty in a particular domain, and the willingness to learn and adapt to new technologies.

The argument for a *full-stack developer* is that, while most developers are either client-side or server-side specialists, a full-stack developer understands both stacks. This argument is rooted in the thought that forcing a strict distinction between the client and server sides discourages developers from learning beyond their specialty, and this artificial boundary prevents them from thinking of a complete end-to-end solution for a problem, thus making them less effective.

Furthermore, expertise is not required at all stages of projects. For example, in the discovery phase, a POC of the system might be required, and having all specialists assigned to this task will bulk up the team size and expense. Small companies and start-ups sometimes need broad domain knowledge and full-stack capabilities to build projects with limited people and resources. Large companies, on the other hand, tend to hire more specialists but can still effectively use full-stack developers for project management as they can visualize the complete system.

No doubt, specialized developers have their own place, but developers with full-stack knowledge help to bridge the gap between the two stacks and have a system-level vision. In a way, full-stack developers complement the work of specialists. Their core value lies in their ability to understand and work on the full breadth of a project.

SWIFT ON SERVER AND VAPOR

Swift is a general-purpose programming language that suits the modern approach to safety, performance, and software design patterns.

Swift has various characteristics that make it suitable for server applications:

- One of the major goals of a modern cloud platform is to maximize resource utilization. Services built with Swift have a very small memory footprint and are also CPU-efficient as compared to other popular server languages with automatic memory management.

- Swift-based applications have a quick start-up time. This makes it a great fit for cloud services, which are often rescheduled onto new VMs or containers to address platform formation changes. It also helps in streamlining continuous delivery pipelines, and quick boot times make it a perfect fit for serverless applications with negligible cold start times.

- Swift's use of ARC and its lack of JIT give it a deterministic performance.

- The Swift server work group promotes the use of Swift for developing and deploying server applications.

- If you come from an iOS background, Swift gives you an edge and a less steep learning curve.

Vapor is a Web framework for Swift that allows us to write back-ends, Web apps, and HTTP servers in Swift.

Vapor shares key practices built up over years of PHP, JavaScript, and Ruby Web framework development, including the **model view controller** (**MVC**) pattern. Just as in iOS, server-side Swift is also a type-safe language. Swift's type safety is enforced by the compiler, and in a Web development context, this differentiates Vapor from modern frameworks based on JavaScript, Rails, PHP, and so on.

Swift's type system might initially feel like it is constricting to developers who are not used to type-safety requirements, but for someone from an iOS background, this will look familiar. Swift's type of safety leads to Web code that is more immune to many of the most common errors in other Web frameworks.

Server-side Swift Web apps are statically compiled and, hence, safer by design. Compiled apps are also more performant relative to their just-in-time-compiled counterparts. A series of benchmarks early in server-side Swift's evolution showed significant performance enhancements relative to common alternatives. For example, the Vapor team presented this platform comparison shortly after the release of Vapor 1, demonstrating superior performance even at that early stage.

Plaintext:

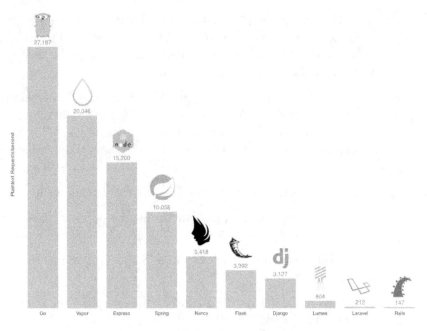

FIGURE 1.4 Plaintext comparison.
*Source: (Server-Side Swift vs. The Other Guys—2: Speed) https://medium.com/@codevapor/
server-side-swift-vs-the-other-guys-2speed-ca65b2f79505*

JSON:

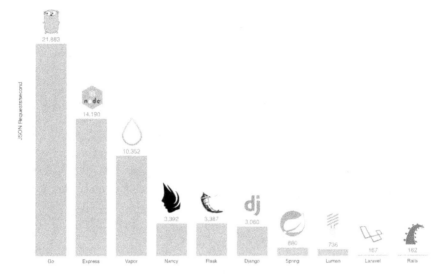

FIGURE 1.5 JSON comparison.

SQLite Fetch:

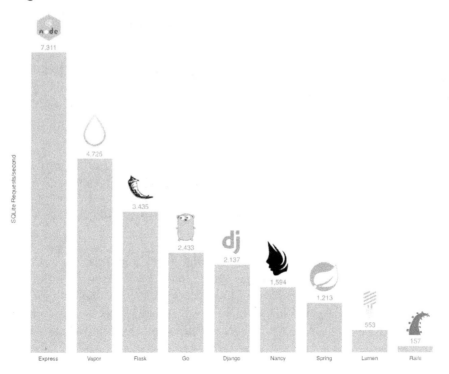

FIGURE 1.6 SQLite Fetch comparison.

However, even if you do not need screaming speed, microservices written in the Vapor framework are typically expected to be exceptionally efficient in their energy and resource use.

SWIFT PACKAGES FOR BACK-END DEVELOPMENT

A tech stack, whether it is dependable or not, can be identified by the community that supports it and how active that community is. Swift Package Manager (SPM) is a great way to distribute Swift packages, and we have so many open-source options to build a back end. Let us go through a list of some of the most widely useful open-source projects that can be used to develop a server application in Swift. Many of these libraries are backed by Apple; therefore, it is an assurance that Apple is supporting them.

SwiftNIO

(*Source: https://github.com/apple/swift-nio*)

SwiftNIO is a cross-platform, event-driven, and asynchronous network application framework used for the rapid development of high-performance and maintainable protocol servers and clients. It is a high-performance and low-level network framework that we can use to build our own server or client using a non-blocking approach.

SwiftNIO is a low-level tool for building high-performance networking applications in Swift. Using SwiftNIO, we can particularly target those use cases where using a *thread-per-connection* model of concurrency is inefficient. This is a common limitation when building servers that use a large number of low-utilization connections, such as HTTP servers.

To achieve these goals, SwiftNIO uses *non-blocking I/O*. Non-blocking I/O differs from the more common blocking I/O model because the application does not need to wait for data to be sent to or received from the network. SwiftNIO asks the kernel to notify it when I/O operations can be performed without waiting.

SwiftNIO does not target providing high-level solutions, for example, Web frameworks. Instead, SwiftNIO's sole focus is on providing the low-level building blocks for these higher-level applications. For building a Web application, most users will not want to use SwiftNIO directly; instead, they will want to use high-level frameworks available in the Swift ecosystem. Those

Web frameworks, however, may choose to use SwiftNIO underneath to provide their networking support.

SwiftNIO is designed as a powerful tool for building networking applications and frameworks, but it does not provide abstraction at all levels. SwiftNIO is highly focused on providing the basic I/O primitives and protocol implementations at low levels of abstraction, thus leaving more expressive and slower abstractions for the wider community to build. The intention here is that SwiftNIO will be a building block for server-side applications, not necessarily the framework for these applications to use directly.

Applications requiring extremely high performance from their networking stack may choose to use SwiftNIO directly in order to reduce overhead, but these applications should be able to maintain extremely high performance with relatively little maintenance cost. SwiftNIO also provides abstractions for this use case. For example, extremely high-performance network servers can be built directly.

The core SwiftNIO repository contains a few extremely important protocol implementations, such as HTTP. The SwiftNIO developer group believes that most protocol implementations should be decoupled from the release cycle of the underlying networking stack, and they encourage the community to develop and maintain their protocol implementations.

AsyncHTTPClient

(*Source: https://github.com/swift-server/async-http-client*)

This package provides an HTTP client library built on top of SwiftNIO. This library provides the following:

- Top-class support for Swift Concurrency (since version 1.9.0)

- The asynchronous and non-blocking architecture of request methods

- Simple follow-redirects and cookie headers are dropped

- Streaming body download

- TLS support

- Automatic HTTP/2 over HTTPS

- Cookie parsing

Swift AWS Lambda Runtime

(*Source: https://github.com/swift-server/swift-aws-lambda-runtime/*)

Many modern software systems have client components, such as iOS, macOS, or watchOS applications, as well as server components with which clients interact. Serverless architecture is often the easiest and most efficient way for client application developers to extend their applications into the cloud.

Serverless architecture is increasingly becoming a popular choice for running event-driven or *ad hoc* computing tasks in the cloud. The power of mission-critical microservices and data-intensive workloads. In many cases, serverless architecture allows developers to easily scale and control computation costs, given their on-demand nature.

When using serverless architecture, special attention must be given to resource utilization, as it directly impacts the costs of the system. This is where Swift helps with its low memory footprint, deterministic performance, and quick start time. Swift is a tremendous match for serverless function architecture.

Combine this with Swift's developer friendliness, expressiveness, and safety, and we have a solution that is great for developers at all skill levels, scalable, and cost-effective.

The Swift AWS Lambda Runtime was designed to make building Lambda functions in Swift simple and safe. This package is an implementation of the AWS Lambda Runtime API and uses an embedded asynchronous HTTP client based on SwiftNIO, which is fine-tuned for performance in the AWS Runtime context. This package provides a multi-tier API that allows the building of a range of Lambda functions, from quick and simple closures to complex, performance-sensitive event handlers.

Soto—AWS SDK Swift

(*Source: https://github.com/soto-project/soto*)

Soto is an SDK written in Swift for **Amazon Web Services** (**AWS**). It works on Linux, macOS, and iOS. This package provides access to all AWS services. The service APIs it provides are a direct mapping of the REST APIs that Amazon publishes for each of its services. Soto is a community-supported project and does not have any affiliation whatsoever with AWS.

The library consists of the following three parts:

1. **Soto-core**, which performs all the core requests on encoding and signing, response decoding, and error handling.

2. The service API files define the individual AWS services and their commands with their input and output structures.

3. The **CodeGenerator** builds the service API files from the JSON model files supplied by Amazon.

CONCLUSION

As we have observed during this chapter, the server-side Swift infrastructure is evolving really fast. Swift is available on all major platforms: Windows, Linux, and Unix.

Why opt for Swift as your main language for the back end? Because Swift is modern, fast, and safe. It is available on all major platforms, and it has a great learning curve. Swift has a bright future not just because of support from Apple but also because of the huge community that supports it.

For someone coming from an iOS background and wanting to go full-stack, Swift and Vapor should be a natural choice because of a relatively easy learning curve and a great support community.

2

SETTING UP THE ENVIRONMENT

INTRODUCTION

Vapor is a Web framework that allows us to write backends, Web app APIs, and HTTP servers in Swift. Vapor is written in Swift, which provides a number of benefits over the more traditional server languages, including being a modern, powerful, and safe language.

We will be exploring full-stack development for iOS in this book; we will only focus on Vapor on macOS and skip Vapor on Linux from the scope of this book.

In this chapter, we will create our first *Hello World* projects in Vapor for the backend and in Swift for iOS. This chapter aims to give a basic understanding of tools and SDKs to start with Vapor and iOS development. In this chapter, we will cover the installation of Xcode, Vapor Toolbox, and starter projects in Vapor as well as for iOS.

STRUCTURE

In this chapter, we will cover the following topics:

* Installation of Xcode
* Installation of Vapor Toolbox
* Hello world project (Vapor)
  * Build and run project
  * Folder structure

- Swift package manager
- Hello World project (iOS)
  - Project structure
  - Run project

INSTALLATION OF XCODE

We need Swift 5.2 or greater to use Vapor on macOS. Swift and all of its dependencies come bundled with Xcode. The minimum required version for working with Vapor on macOS is Xcode 11.4:

1. To install Xcode, proceed to the **Mac App Store** and install the latest version of **Xcode**, as shown in the following figure:

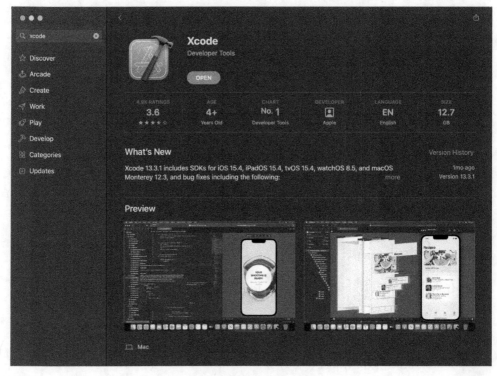

FIGURE 2.1 Install Xcode.

2. After Xcode has been downloaded, open it to complete the installation. This will take a while.

3. Open the terminal and check Swift's version:

```
swift --version
```

4. You will see Swift's version information printed on the terminal, as follows:

```
swift-driver version: 1.45.2 Apple Swift version 5.6
(swiftlang-5.6.0.323.62 clang-1316.0.20.8)

Target: x86_64-apple-macosx12.0
```

INSTALLATION OF THE VAPOR TOOLBOX

1. As we have Swift installed, let us install the Vapor toolbox. The Vapor toolbox is distributed through Homebrew. If you do not have Homebrew installed, first install Homebrew. Open the terminal and run the following command to install Homebrew:

```
$ /bin/bash -c "$(curl -fsSL https://raw.githubusercontent.com/
Homebrew/install/HEAD/install.sh)"
```

2. It is time to install the Vapor toolbox:

```
brew install vapor
```

3. Run the help command to double-check that the installation of the Vapor toolbox is successful and to list the available commands:

```
vapor --help
```

4. You will see the output on the terminal, as shown in the following figure:

```
Usage: vapor <command>

Vapor Toolbox (Server-side Swift web framework)

Commands:
      build Builds an app in the console.
      clean Cleans temporary files.
     heroku Commands for working with Heroku.
        new Generates a new app.
        run Runs an app from the console.
            Equivalent to `swift run Run`.
            The --enable-test-discovery flag is automatically set if needed.
 supervisor Commands for working with supervisord.
      xcode Opens an app in Xcode.

Use `vapor <command> [--help,-h]` for more information on a command.
hdutt@HDUTT-M-40QV ~ % 
```

FIGURE 2.2 Vapor Help.

HELLO WORLD PROJECT (VAPOR)

1. As we have installed Xcode and Vapor, continuing the customary tradition of the programming world, we will create a Hello World project. Open the terminal and use the Vapor Toolbox's new project command as follows:

    ```
    vapor new Hello -n
    ```

    The -n flag creates a bare-bones template by automatically answering no to all questions.

2. This will create a new folder in the current directory with the project, as shown in the following figure:

FIGURE 2.3 Hello World.

3. Change the directory to the newly created folder in the terminal:

    ```
    cd Hello
    ```

Build and Run Project

1. Open the project in Xcode by running the following command:

    ```
    open Package.swift
    ```

2. This command will automatically start downloading the Swift Package Manager dependencies. This will take some time, as this is the first time you are opening the project. After the dependency resolution is complete,

Xcode will populate the available schemes and open the project, as shown in the following figure:

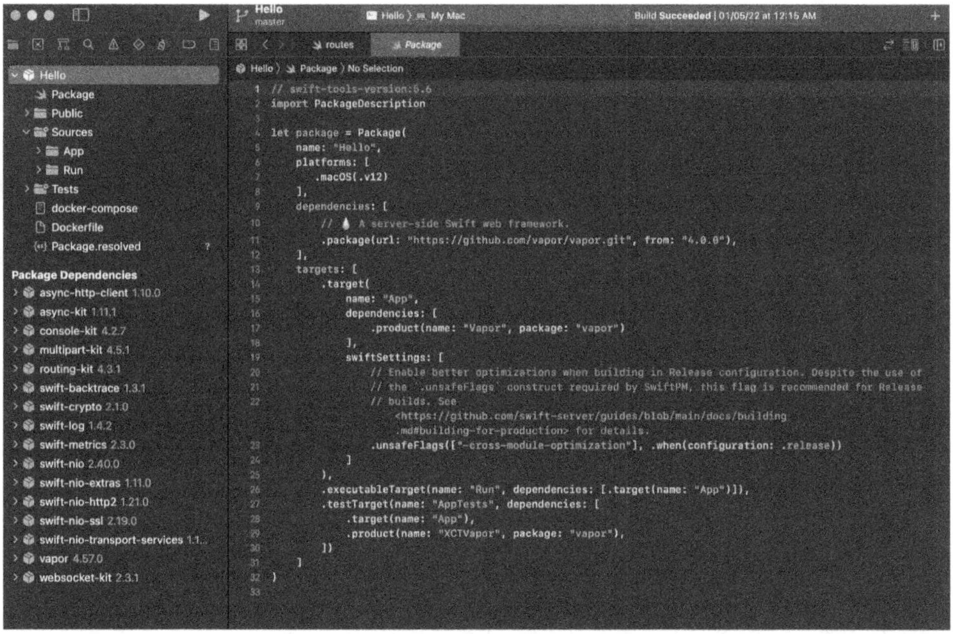

FIGURE 2.4 Open project.

3. At the top of the Xcode window, to the right of the **Play** and **Stop** buttons, click on the project name to select the project's scheme if not already selected, and run **Target**, **My Mac**. Click the **Play** button to build and run the project.

    We should see the console output at the bottom of the Xcode window, as shown in the following figure:

[NOTICE] Server starting on http://127.0.0.1:8080

FIGURE 2.5 Console output.

4. Open your Web browser and visit **http://127.0.0.1:8080** or **localhost:8080**. You should see the page shown in the following figure:

FIGURE 2.6 Browser output.

5. If we visit **http://127.0.0.1:8080/hello** or **localhost: 8080/hello**, you should see the page shown in the following figure:

FIGURE 2.7 Hello World Output.

Folder Structure

As we have created and built our "**Hello World**" in the Vapor app, let us familiarize ourselves with the project's folder structure, which is based on **SPM's** folder structure. See the following figure:

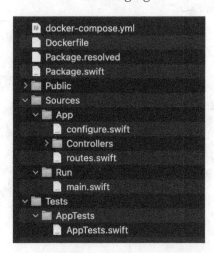

FIGURE 2.8 Folder structure.

Public Folder

This folder contains all the public files that will be served by the Vapor app if **FileMiddleware** is enabled. These files are usually images, style sheets, browser scripts, and so on. We need to enable **FileMiddleware** in the **configure.swift** file to make Vapor serve public files.

```
// configures your application

public func configure(_ app: Application) throws {

    // Serve files from /Public folder

    app.middleware.use(FileMiddleware(publicDirectory:
    app.directory.publicDirectory))


    // register routes

    try routes(app)

}
```

Sources

The **sources** folder contains all Swift source files for the project. The top-level folders are **App** and **Run**. The **App** folder is where all the application logic goes. Within the **App** folder, the **Controllers** folder should be used for grouping together application logic. Most controllers have functions that accept a request and return a response.

The file **configure.swift** contains the **configure(_:)** function, which is called by **main.swift** to configure the newly created **Application**. This is where we should register services such as routes, databases, providers, and so on.

The **routes.swift** file contains the **routes(_:)** method, which is called near the end of **configure(_:)** to register routes to the **Application**.

Run

This is the main executable target. This contains just the code needed to get the application up and running. The **main.swift** file creates and runs a configured instance of the Vapor application.

Tests

Every module in the **Sources** folder should have a corresponding folder in **Tests**. This contains test cases built on the **XCTest** module for testing the package. The **AppTests** folder contains the unit tests for code in the **App** module.

SWIFT PACKAGE MANAGER

The Swift Package Manager (SPM) is used for building the project's source code and dependencies. As Vapor relies heavily on SPM, let us just understand the basics of SPM.

It is similar to Cocoapods or NPM. It can be used from the command line or with compatible IDEs. However, it does not have a central package index for SPM packages. It leverages URLs to Git repositories and version dependencies using Git tags.

The first place **SPM** looks in the project is the package manifest. This file should always be located in the **root** directory of the project and named **Package.swift**, as shown in the following figure:

FIGURE 2.9 Package manifest.

The first line of the package manifest indicates the minimum version of Swift that the package supports. The first argument to **Package** is the package's name. If the **package** is public, it should be the last segment of the Git repo's URL as the name.

The platform array specifies which platforms this package supports. By specifying **.macOS(.v12);** this package requires macOS Mojave or greater. When Xcode loads this project, it will automatically set the minimum deployment version to macOS 12.

Dependencies are SPM packages other than those your package relies on. All Vapor applications rely on the Vapor package, but we can add other dependencies as well. In *Figure 2.9*, we observe that vapor version 4.0.0 or later is a dependency of this package.

The **targets** specify all of the modules, executables, and tests that the package contains. Most Vapor apps have three targets, but we can add as many as we like to organize the code. Each target declares which modules it depends on. We need to add module names here to be able to import them into the code. A target can depend on other targets in the project or on modules exposed by packages we have added to the main dependencies array.

While building a project for the first time, SPM creates a **Package. resolved** file that stores the version of each dependency. To update the dependencies, run a Swift package update.

For Xcode 11 or greater, changes to dependencies, targets, products, and so on will happen automatically whenever the **Package.swift** file is modified.

HELLO WORLD PROJECT (IOS)

1. To create our first Hello World project for iOS, launch Xcode again. You will arrive at Xcode's welcome page, where you can click on the **Create a new Xcode Project** link to start creating a new project, as shown in the following figure:

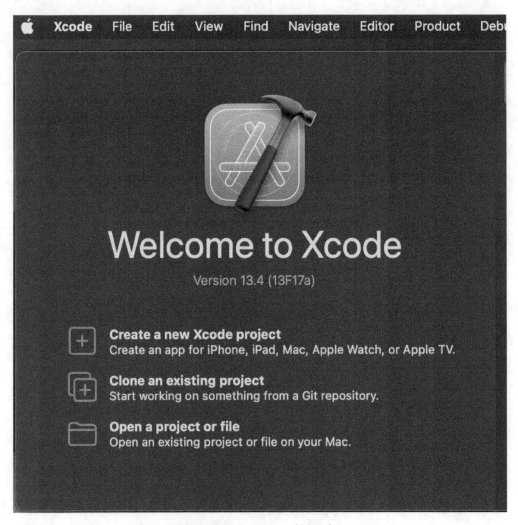

FIGURE 2.10 Create a new iOS project.

2. After clicking on **Create a new Xcode Project**, you will arrive at the next page, where you can select the platform, such as iOS, macOS, watchOS, and so on, for your **Hello World** project. Select **iOS** from the platform list and select **App** as a template, as shown in the following figure:

FIGURE 2.11 Select the iOS project template.

3. After selecting the platform and template, you will arrive at the next page, where you will be able to name your project. For this sample, we will name the project **Hello World**, as shown in *Figure 2.12*.

4. At this point, you do not need to add the Team; therefore, we can leave it untouched.

5. In the organizer identifier, you can use the reverse domain name of your organization, like **com.yourCompanyName**.

6. For the interface, use Storyboard, and for language, choose Swift.

7. We do not need Core Data and Unit Test cases for this sample project; therefore, we will keep them unchecked.

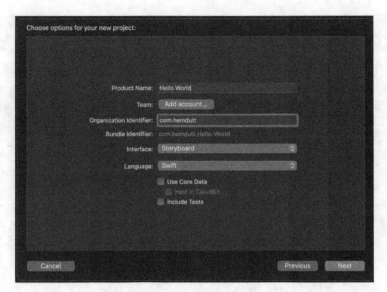

FIGURE 2.12 Project configuration.

8. Click on the **Next** button and select a directory to save your project. As soon as you click on the **Next** button, a modal window will appear to select a directory for the project. In this window, you can navigate to the desired directory location on the machine and save the project, as shown in the following figure:

FIGURE 2.13 Select project directory.

9. As soon as you click on the **Create** button, Xcode will create a new project in the directory, as shown in the following figure:

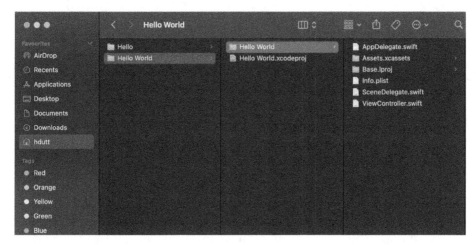

FIGURE 2.14 New project.

Project Structure

Let us discuss the project structure of our newly created **Hello World** project:

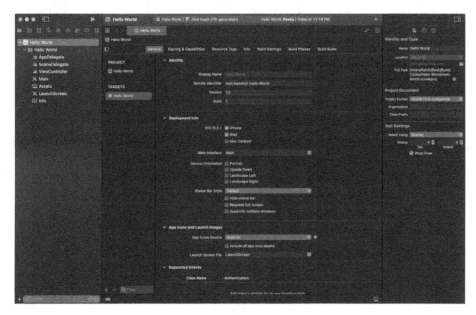

FIGURE 2.15 Project structure.

As shown in the preceding figure, the first two files in the project structure are **AppDelegate** and **SceneDelegate**. **AppDelegate** is responsible for the application lifecycle and setup, whereas **SceneDelegate** is responsible for what is shown on the screen (Windows or Scenes) and handles and manages the way your app is shown.

In all iOS apps, **AppDelegate** is the main entry point for the app, and it is the place for handling app states. From iOS 13, as a result of the new multi-window support feature that is introduced with iPad-OS, **SceneDelegate** is introduced to handle Windows and Scenes.

ViewController is the default view controller created in the project template. **Main. storyboard** is the default storyboard provided by the template. We will add our **Hello World** label here.

The **Assets** folder holds the image assets required in the application bundle. **LaunchScreen.storyboard** is the very first screen presented to the user on **App** launch. Generally, the company logo or similar branding stuff is presented on this screen.

To provide a better experience for users, iOS and macOS rely on the presence of special metadata in each app or bundle. **Info.plist** is a configuration file that holds this metadata. This metadata is used in many different ways. Some of it is displayed to the user, some of it is used internally by the system to identify your app and the document types it supports, and some of it is used by the system frameworks to facilitate the launch of apps.

Add Hello World Label

Let us create the UI for our **Hello World** project. Click on **Main. storyboard**, as shown in the following figure:

1. In the right panel, you will see **ViewController** Scene. Expanding the scene will show the View Controller hierarchy, which by default contains a view where we can place the UI elements. Furthermore, notice that in the following figure, the rightmost panel shows an iPhone-like screen, where we can design and visualize the UI before launching the simulator.

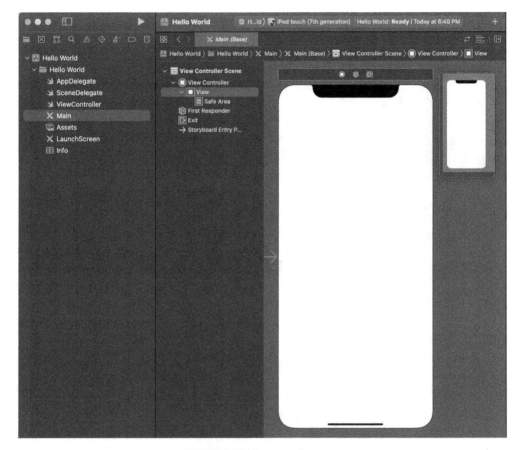

FIGURE 2.16 View controller scene.

2. Next, as shown in the following figure, click on the **+** button at the right-most top corner to open the window and browse the available UI objects. For our **Hello World** project, we need a static string; therefore, a **Label** would be a good choice.

3. Click on the search field and type **Label** to access the label object for the UI.

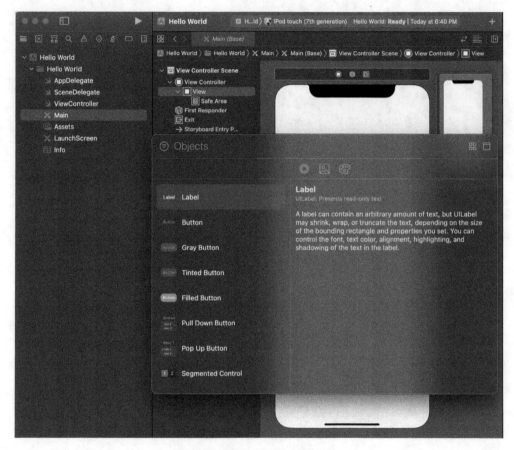

FIGURE 2.17 UI object library.

4. Drag the **Label** object from the browser window and place it on the iPhone screen below. Drag the label onto the iPhone screen to place it at your desired place on the screen. We will drag it to the center of the screen for our example, as shown in *Figure 2.18*.

5. Double-click or press the *Enter* key on the **Label**, which will become editable. Type **Hello World** in the **Label** object.

6. Notice that when you add **Label** to the screen, it also updates the **ViewController** scene hierarchy as well. Notice that a **Label** is added as a child of the View Controller's view.

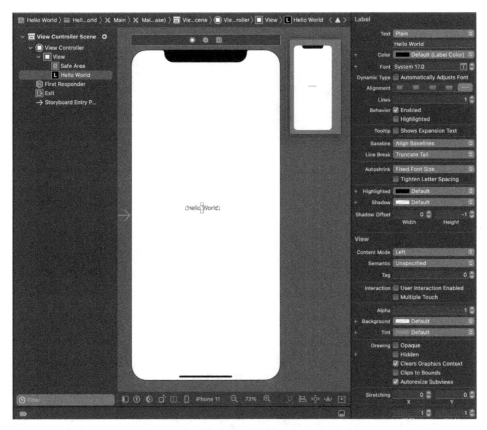

FIGURE 2.18 UI design.

7. The rightmost panel is the attribute inspector, where you can view and customize the UI element's property. In this case, you can see that **Label** has various customizable properties, such as text color, background color, and text truncation behavior, among others. You can play with these properties to see how they affect the UI of the label.

RUN XCODE PROJECT

1. Since we are done with the basic **Hello World** label UI, let us prepare to run this project. Refer to the figure below.

2. At the Xcode top bar, you will see a target **Hello World** (highlighted with the red circle in the figure). If you do not see this target, click on the **Link** and select this **Target**.

3. Next to the target, there is a link for selecting the simulator for testing the code.

FIGURE 2.19 Set up run environment.

4. As is evident in *Figure 2.19*, the simulator selected by default is the iPod touch. If you click on this link, it will open a drop-down list of all available Simulator options in Xcode. Refer to the following figure:

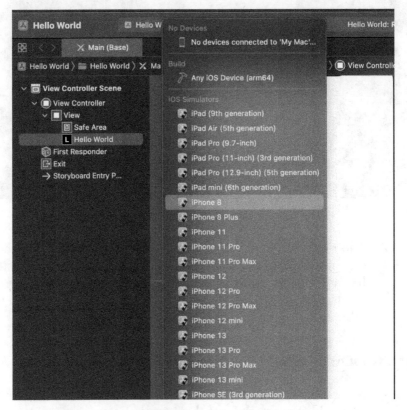

FIGURE 2.20 Simulator options.

5. After all this hard work, it is time to run the project. Refer to the following figure: At the top bar of Xcode, you will see a **Play** button (highlighted with the red circle in the figure):

FIGURE 2.21 Run project.

6. Press the **Play** button to run the project. This will first build the project and then launch the selected **iPhone Simulator**, as shown in the following figure:

FIGURE 2.22 iPhone simulator.

7. After a few seconds, our app will launch and display the "**Hello World**" text on UI. See the following figure:

FIGURE 2.23 App launch.

8. As evident from the title bar of the simulator, it bears the designation of **iPhone 8**, which is our chosen simulator. Furthermore, notice that during design, we placed **Label** in the center; it is not in the center in the simulator. At the top right corner of the Simulator title bar, there is a **rotation** icon. Click on this icon to rotate the phone into **Layout** mode, as shown in the following figure:

FIGURE 2.24 Simulator layout mode.

9. As is evident, as soon as we rotated the Simulator, the `Hello World` Label was not visible. This issue and the first issue we discussed where the `Label` is not center aligned have the same root cause, and that is because we have not handled Auto Layout yet.

We will read in detail about Auto Layout in the upcoming chapters. For the time being, let us enjoy our success and run our first `Hello World` project.

CONCLUSION

In this chapter, we covered the installation of Xcode and Vapor Toolbox, which are essential tools to start with Swift for server and iOS development. We also covered creating a starter project with Vapor for the server and a starter project for iOS, along with their respective folders and project structures.

In the upcoming chapters, we will dive deep into the concepts of server development in Vapor and iOS application development.

ROUTING, MVC, AND JSON IN VAPOR

INTRODUCTION

In this chapter, we will go through the basics of creating a Web API using Vapor and the fundamentals of working with routes. We will also explore how to create controllers in Vapor to implement the **Model View Controller** (**MVC**) design pattern. Later, we will learn about working with JSON with Vapor APIs.

STRUCTURE

In this chapter, we will cover the following topics:

- Routes
- Router methods
  - Basic routes
  - Nested routes
  - Route parameters
  - Anything routes and CatchAll routes
  - Query strings
  - Route groups
- Model-View-Controller (MVC)
- Working with JSON
  - Posting JSON and Postman app

OBJECTIVES

This chapter aims to give a basic understanding of creating Routes for the server application, a brief understanding of the MVC design pattern, and creating Controllers in a Vapor application. We will also explore the JSON format and handling JSON in a Vapor app and extend this discussion. We will also cover the Postman app for testing the Routes.

ROUTES

The first question that comes to mind when one hears *Route* is: What are Routes? Routes are also known as API endpoints. Therefore, if someone is talking about routes or API endpoints, the person basically means the same exact thing. A Route or API endpoint is basically a URL to a resource. This means that you will hit a particular route and get some results from it. It could be a list of movies, a list of restaurants near you, or the menu of your favorite restaurant.

Therefore, if we are building a **Restaurant** lister API and we want to create a new route that will give us all the **Restaurants**, we can write a route that will look something like the following: *https://www.mydomain.com/restaurants*.

Generally, when people talk about routes, they only talk about the last part. The domain name, **mydomain**, in this case, is pretty much the same for all the different routes or API endpoints.

Therefore, in a nutshell, routing is the process of finding the right request handler for the incoming service request. At the core of Vapor's routing is **RoutingKit** (*https://github.com/vapor/routing-kit*).

Before going further into the details of routing, let us first understand the basics of HTTP requests. Let us again take a look at our route: *https://www.mydomain.com/restaurants*. This is a simple **GET** request for which the browser will make a request like the following:

```
GET /restaurants HTTP/1.1

host: mydomain

content-length: 0
```

The first part of the request is the HTTP method. **GET** is the most common HTTP method, but there are several others that we will use often. These HTTP methods are often associated with CRUD semantics, as shown in the following table (*Table 3.1*):

TABLE 3.1 HTTP methods and CRUD.

Method	CRUD	Route example
GET	Read	*https://www.mydomain.com/restaurants*
POST	Create	*https://www.mydomain.com/restaurants*
PUT	Replace	*https://www.mydomain.com/restaurants/Id*
PATCH	Update	*https://www.mydomain.com/restaurants/Id*
DELETE	Delete	*https://www.mydomain.com/restaurants/Id*

Right after the HTTP method comes the request's URI. A URI consists of a path starting with a **/** and an optional query string after **?**. The combination of the HTTP method and path is used to route requests.

ROUTER METHODS

Let us look at the various router methods of Vapor:

Basic Routes

Since we know what the Routes are, let us go ahead and start creating some very basic routes. However, before that, let us create a new Vapor project, which we will enhance and continue to work on during the course of this book.

1. As described in *Chapter 2, Setting Up the Environment,* follow the steps to create a new project by typing the following Vapor command in the terminal:

```
vapor new VaporApp -n
```

2. Then launch the project by typing the following commands in the same terminal window:

```
cd VaporApp

open package.swift
```

3. Next, in the project hierarchy, open **Sources** | **App** | **routes.swift** file, as shown in the following figure:

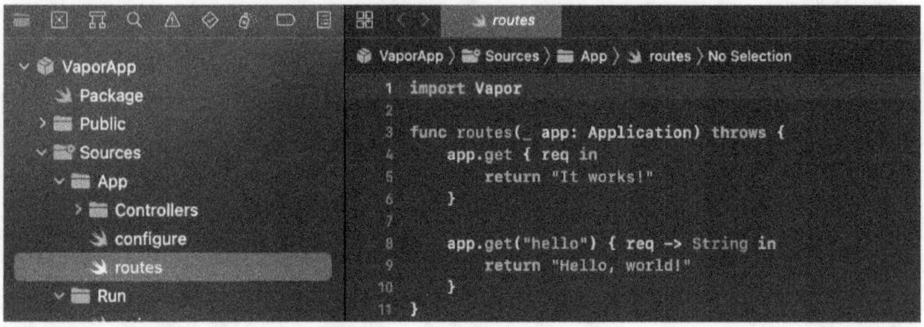

FIGURE 3.1 Routes.

4. As is evident, there are two routes already created by the template by default. We will remove these template routes and start anew. However, first, let us understand what these routes are.

5. The first route is a root route that takes a request in and returns a string **It works!**. We have already tested this route in our **Hello World** project. This route can be accessed by visiting **http://localhost:8080**.

6. Another example of the template function is a route with a name; in this case, the route name is **hello**. This route can be accessed at **http://localhost:8080/hello**.

Nested Routes

In the section, *Basic Routes*, we learned about the **root** route and the **named** route. However, in our daily lives, we do not encounter such simple URLs. For example, what if you want to get the best restaurants with a specialty in Chinese food? We cannot create root routes for such requests. The answer to this is nested routes.

Therefore, for our restaurant query, the URL would be something like the following: **http://localhost:8080/restaurants/specialty/chinese**.

One immediate thought that comes to mind is that it would be possible to create a route like the following:

```
app.get("restaurants/specialty/chinese") { req -> String in

}
```

However, Vapor syntax does not work like this. To create such a route, we have to pass in multiple parameters, like the following:

```
app.get("restaurants", "specialty", "chinese") { req -> String
in return "restaurants/specialty/chinese"

}
```

Let us run this code and see if this route works or not.

1. Click on the play button on Xcode to run the project, as shown in the following figure:

FIGURE 3.2 Nested routes.

2. As soon as you see **[NOTICE] Server starting at http://127.0.0.1:8080** on the Xcode console screen, as shown in the following figure, we can test the nested route in the browser:

FIGURE 3.3 Starting server.

3. Open the browser, and in the address bar, type **http://local-host:8080/restaurants/specialty/chinese**. You should see a string **restaurants/specialty/Chinese** on the Web screen, as shown in the following figure:

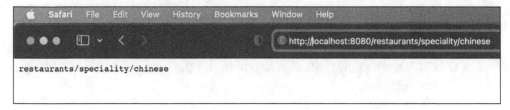

FIGURE 3.4 Nested route.

Hence, the obvious question that comes to our curious minds is that a specialty could be anything; it could be **Chinese** or **Indian** or **Thai** or **French**, and so on.

One way of handling this is to create multiple functions for each specialty, like the following examples:

```
app.get("restaurants", "specialty", "indian") { req -> String in return
       "restaurants/specialty/indian"

}
```

```
app.get("restaurants", "specialty", "thai") { req -> String in return
       "restaurants/specialty/thai"

}
```

If we run the project and access these routes, it will give us the desired results, as shown in the following figure:

FIGURE 3.5 Indian cuisine.

And in the following figure:

FIGURE 3.6 Thai cuisine.

However, as any experienced developer would know, this solution is not scalable, as this means having hundreds of APIs for this trivial feature.

Therefore, what is the solution? Let us explore this in the next section.

Route Parameters

Let us revisit the problem statement from the last section. We want to create an API endpoint that can take a variable **specialty** parameter; therefore, we do not have to hardcode a bunch of routes just to get the best restaurants for a particular **specialty**.

Therefore, our API should look something like the following: **http://localhost:8080/restaurants/specialty/region**, where the region is variable.

In Vapor, we can write this route as follows:

```
//http://localhost:8080/restaurants/specialty/region

app.get("restaurants", "specialty", ":region") { req -> String in

    guard let region = req.parameters.get("region") else {

        throw Abort(.badRequest)

    }

    return "restaurants/specialty/\(region)"

}
```

At this point, if you notice, in **app.get**, we have three parameters; the first two parameters, **restaurants** and **specialty** are nested routes, whereas the third parameter, **:region**, is a route parameter. Delete the three routes we created in the last section, *Nested Routes*, and now our **routes.swift** will look as shown in the following figure:

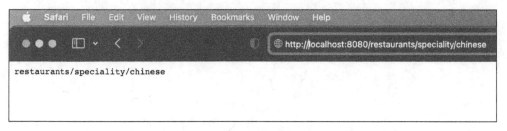

```
import Vapor

func routes(_ app: Application) throws {

    //http://localhost:8080
    app.get { req in
        return "It works!"
    }

    //http://localhost:8080/hello
    app.get("hello") { req -> String in
        return "Hello, world!"
    }

    //http://localhost:8080/restaurants/speciality/region
    app.get("restaurants", "speciality", ":region") { req -> String in
        guard let region = req.parameters.get("region") else {
            throw Abort(.badRequest)
        }
        return "restaurants/speciality/\(region)"
    }
}
```

FIGURE 3.7 Route parameter.

To test our route parameter, run the project, and when you see the message **[NOTICE] Server starting at http://127.0.0.1:8080** in the console, open **Browser** and type **http://127.0.0.1:8080/restaurants/specialty/chinese** in the address bar. You should see a Web page, as shown in the following figure:

restaurants/speciality/chinese

FIGURE 3.8 Parameterized routes.

You can try more URLs, like **http://localhost:8080/restaurants/specialty/french**, **http://localhost:8080/restaurants/specialty/italian**, and so on, to validate the route.

Let us see what will happen if we have multiple variable parameters for a route. For example, if we want to search for a restaurant with a specialty in a particular place, how would we go about it?

For example, we need an API that will look something like: **http://localhost/restaurants/delhi/specialty/italian**, **http://localhost/restaurants/newyork/specialty/italian**, and so on.

To implement such an API, we will go about it with the same approach as mentioned in the previous example, with a slight variation as follows:

```
//http://localhost:8080/restaurants/state/location/specialty/region

app.get("restaurants", ":location", "specialty", ":region") { req ->
String in

   guard let location = req.parameters.get("location"), let
region = req.parameters.get("region") else {

     throw Abort(.badRequest)

}

return "restaurants in \(location) with specialty \(region)"

}
```

Our **routes.swift** file will look as shown in the following figure:

FIGURE 3.9 Multiple route parameters.

Let us test this. **Run** the project, and as you see the message **[NOTICE] Server starting at http://127.0.0.1:8080** in the console, launch the browser, and in the address bar, type **http://localhost:8080/ restaurants/state/newyork/specialty/italian**. You should see a Web page as shown in the following figure:

restaurants in newyork with speciality italian

FIGURE 3.10 Route with two parameters.

This is great so far. However, what if we want to match anything, kind of like a wildcard?

Therefore, in a way, we want to create some sort of wildcard parameter where people can just pass on anything they want. How?

Anything Routes and Catch-All Routes

In this section, we will cover two more cases and two more different ways in which you can create routes. One is called the anything route, and the other is called the catch-all route.

First, let us talk about exactly what anything route is.

Anything route basically means that, for example, if your route is **route-any/bar/endpoint** or **routeany/xyz/endpoint**, then the middle part, that is, **bar** or **xyz**, could be anything. Therefore, let us see how we can create a route for such cases.

```
//Anything route

app.get("routeany", "*", "endpoint") { req -> String in return
"This is anything route"

}
```

* represents that you can pass anything in that parameter. Let us now run this code and see how it works.

Furthermore, press the **Play** button on your Xcode, and when you see the message **[NOTICE] Server starting at http://127.0.0.1:8080** in the console, open the browser and test anything route with different parameters, as shown in the following figure:

FIGURE 3.11 Anything Route 1.

And in the following figure:

FIGURE 3.12 Anything Route 2.

The catch-all route is similar, but in this case, the whole remaining part of the route, which comes after **routeany**, can be replaced with anything.

Therefore, an example of that route could be where we have routes **routeany/xyz** and **routeany/xyz/bar**. Let us see how we can create such a route:

```
//CatchAll route

app.get("routeany", "**") { req -> String in
    return "This is Catch-all route"

}
```

** represents that you can pass anything in that parameter. Let us now run this code and see how it works.

Furthermore, press the **Play** button on your Xcode, and when you see the message **[NOTICE] Server starting at http://127.0.0.1:8080** in the console, open the browser and test anything routes with different parameters, as shown in the following figure:

FIGURE 3.13 Catch-all Route 1.

And in *Figure 3.14: Catch-all Route 2*:

FIGURE 3.14 Catch-all Route 2.

Query Strings

Let us talk about how we can access query string values when we are using Vapor in situations like the following:

Let us assume that we have some sort of route search, and then we specify the keyword that we are searching for and let us assume we are searching for Italian food, and the page number for that is 10 or something. In this case, the URL will look like the following:

http://localhost:8080/search?keyword=italian&page=10

Therefore, in this case, we have two different query string values, which are a keyword and the page number. The value is **Italian** for the keyword and **10** for the page.

The following steps will guide you on how to access these values when we are using Vapor:

1. A route for this sort of requirement can be created as follows:

```
//http://localhost:8080/search?keyword=italian&page=10    app.
get("search") { req -> String in

    guard let keyword = req.query["keyword"] as String?, let page
    ·= req.query["page"] as String? else {
        throw Abort(.badRequest)
    }

    return "Search for Keyword \(keyword) on Page \(page)"

}
```

2. Furthermore, press the **Play** button on your Xcode, and when you see the message **[NOTICE] Server starting at http://127.0.0.1:8080** in the console, open the **Browser,** and test query parameters with different parameters shown as follows:

FIGURE 3.15 Query Strings 1.

3. Change the page number in the query string to 21 and refresh the page.

FIGURE 3.16 Query Strings 2.

4. Change the keyword in the query string to **french** and refresh the page.

FIGURE 3.17 Query Strings 3.

Route Groups

Let us talk about route groups, what they are, and how they can help you organize your route better in Vapor. Let us revisit the examples discussed in sections *Basic routes*, *Nested routes*, and *Route parameters*. Assuming we have to reorganize the following routes:

```
/restaurants
```

```
/restaurants/specialty/region
```

Route groups basically allow you to create a prefix. As we can see from the preceding routes, **restaurants** are the prefix. So, any route we are going to create for restaurants will begin with **restaurants**.

Let us create a group for this as follows:

```
let restaurants = app.grouped("restaurants")
```

Therefore, if we want to create a base route that will look like: **http://local-host:8080/restaurants**, we will create a route like the following:

```
restaurants.get { req -> String in

return "restaurants base route"

}
```

Furthermore, if we want to create a parameterized route like: **http://localhost:8080/restaurants/starRating/5**, we will create a route like the following:

```
restaurants.get("starRating", ":stars") { req -> String in
    guard let stars = req.parameters.get("stars") else {

        throw Abort(.badRequest)

    }

    return "restaurants/starRating/\(stars)"

}
```

Press the **Play** button on your Xcode, and when you see the message **[NOTICE] Server starting at http://127.0.0.1:8080** in the console, open the browser and test route groups for different routes shown as follows:

FIGURE 3.18 Route Groups 1.

Refer to the following figure:

FIGURE 3.19 Route Groups 2.

With this, we can conclude our discussion on Routes. Now is the time to understand some basic design patterns and other nuances of Swift Vapor.

MODEL-VIEW-CONTROLLER (MVC)

MVC is a software development pattern that divides software architecture into the following three main components:

1. *Model*: A model is a class where your data resides. Things such as persistence, model objects, parsers, managers, and networking code live there.

2. *View*: The view layer is the user interface of your app. It is what users see on the screen. Its classes are often reusable as they do not contain any domain-specific logic.

3. *Controller*: The controller is a mediator class between the view and the model via delegation pattern. All the business logic resides here. A model communicates its state to the view layer via the controller, and vice versa.

When put together, this system looks like, as shown in the following figure:

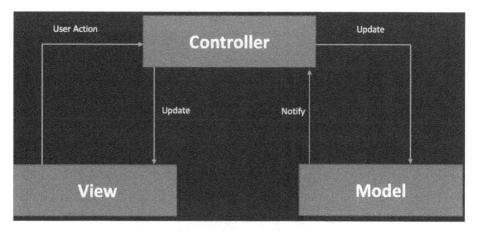

FIGURE 3.20 MVC.

MVC is a design pattern, not a strict rule to which you must always adhere. Use MVC and other design patterns as needed as architectural guidelines and foundations for your app.

In the previous sections covering the basics of Routes, we wrote all the route handlers in **routes.swift**. This, of course, is not sustainable for large projects, as the file will quickly become too big to handle.

In this section, we will introduce the MVC pattern in our project to help manage our routes and models.

As described above, MVC is a design pattern, and therefore, controllers in Vapor serve a similar purpose to controllers in iOS. They handle interactions with a client, such as requests, process them, and return the response. This provides a way of organizing the code in a better way. Following the MVC practice, we will have all interactions with a model on a dedicated controller.

The MVC pattern was also used, making it easy to organize the application. For example, there could be one controller to manage an older version of the APIs and another to manage the current version. This allows the separation of responsibilities in the code and keeps it maintainable.

Therefore, let us get started with our first controller. Open the terminal, navigate to the project directory, and open the Xcode project.

1. Open **Package.swift**.

2. Now create a new Swift file as shown in the following figure:

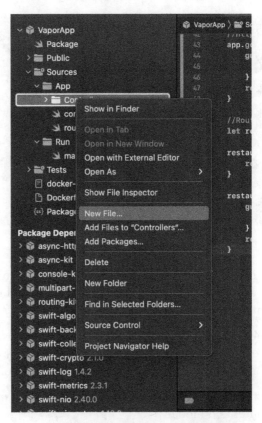

FIGURE 3.21 Create a new controller.

3. After clicking on the **New File** in the **Context** menu, select **Swift file** and name it **UserController** for example, as shown in the following figure:

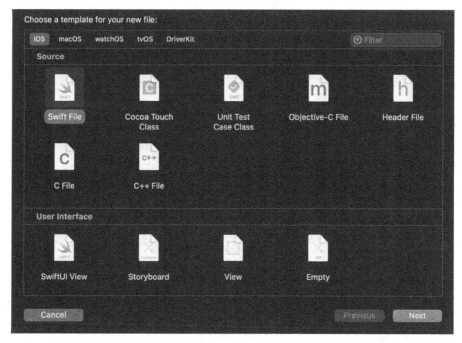

FIGURE 3.22 New Swift file.

4. A new file will be created under the **Controller** folder, as shown in the following:

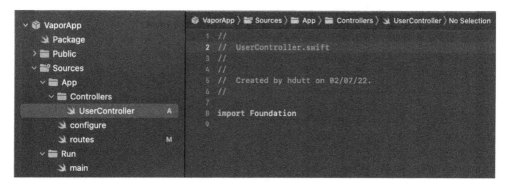

FIGURE 3.23 UserController.

5. Import Vapor into the controller file. Thereafter, let us look into the details of creating routes in the Controller.

6. Inside the Controller, we will define different route handlers. To access these routes, we need to register these handlers with the router. A crude way to do this is to call the functions inside the Controller from **routes. swift**. For example:

```
app.get(

    "api",

    "Users",

    use: userController. getAllUsers)
```

This example calls **getAllUsers (_:)** on the **userController**. Instead of passing a closure as the final parameter, you pass the function to use.

This approach works well for small applications. However, if we have a large number of routes to register, **routes.swift** again becomes unmanageable. It is good practice to make controllers responsible for registering the routes they control. Vapor provides the protocol **RouteCollection** to enable this.

Therefore, we are going to go ahead and create a structure, which is called **UserController**, and it will conform to **RouteCollection**. As discussed, we will be using a **RouteCollection** inside this Controller and will implement all of our roots.

```
struct UserController : RouteCollection {



}
```

As soon as we confirm **UserController** to **RouteCollection**, there is an error indicating that Controller is not really conforming to **RouteCollection**, as shown in the following figure.

If we need to conform to the **RouteCollection** successfully, we need to implement the boot function. Click on the **fix** button on the error box shown in the following figure, and this will add the **boot** function to the Controller:

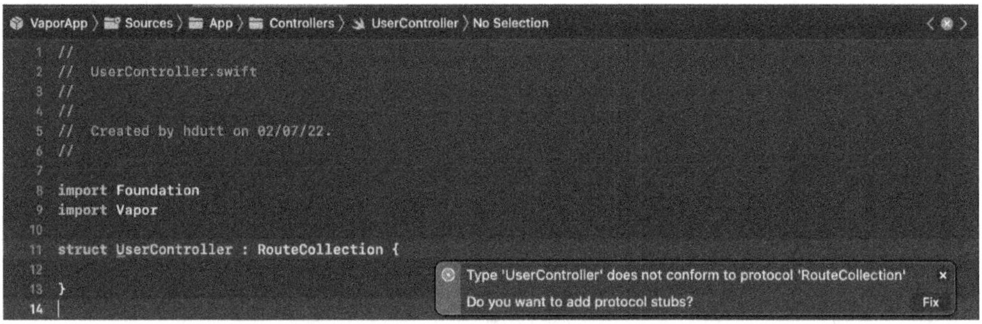

FIGURE 3.24 RouteCollection conforms to error.

The boot has parameter routes, which is a **RouteBuilder**, and you can use these routes to create your routes:

```
struct UserController : RouteCollection {
    func boot(routes: RoutesBuilder) throws {

    }

}
```

We will go ahead and use the grouping feature, which we learned about in earlier sections.

1. We will create a group for **users** so that all the routes in the Controller that we are going to create will be assigned to the users.

2. Create a function in the Controller, named **getAllUsers**, which will take a Request, throw an exception, and let us make it return a string.

```
func getAllUsers(request: Request) throws -> String {

}
```

3. Currently, let us just return a constant string: **All Users**.

```
func getAllUsers(request: Request) throws -> String {
    return "All Users"

}
```

4. Let us also create a route for this function in the **boot** function:

```
func boot(routes: RoutesBuilder) throws {

    //users Group
```

```
let users = routes.grouped("users")

//Routes

users.get(use: getAllUsers)

}
```

5. We still need to connect all these things together. That is, we still have to tell the Vapor application that we are using **UserController** for the / user route group.

    Therefore, how can we do that?

6. Let us get out of this Controller and open **routes.swift** file, and inside the route file, you can see that the app is already passed.

7. We can simply use the register function of the app; when you type that, you can see that it takes in a **RouteCollection** type of parameter, as shown in the following figure:

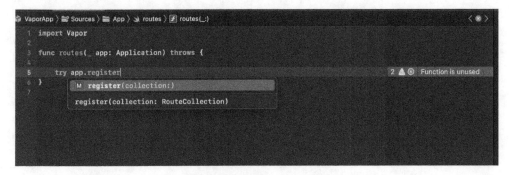

FIGURE 3.25 Register Controller.

8. Because our **UserController** conforms to this protocol, we can simply pass in the **UserController**.

```
func routes(_ app: Application) throws {

    try app.register(collection: UserController())

}
```

And make sure that you call the **register** function with a try because it is a throwable function.

9. It is time to check out our first route. We will proceed to run the server, and once the server is running, we can simply visit **http://local-host:8080/users**. This is going to trigger the **UserController**, and it is going to take this particular route as shown in the following figure:

FIGURE 3.26 All users.

`What if we want to create routes to go to a particular user ID? Where would the second part be the route parameter?

Therefore, let us see how we can build that. We are going to go ahead and create a group.

```
// /user/userId users.group(":userId") { user in
    user.get(use: show)
}
```

10. In this group, we are grouping all the routes that lead to the user ID. The **get** function here will call the **show** function when the user ID is passed in the route, such as **http://localhost:8080/users/123**.

11. Now let us create the show function like the following:

```
func show(request: Request) throws -> String {
guard let userId = request.parameters.get("userId") as
    String? else {
    throw Abort(.badRequest)
}
return "Show user for user id = \(userId)"
}
```

12. In the **show** function, we can extract the user ID value from the request parameter.

13. Let us go ahead and stop the server and start the server again to test our new route. This time we are going to go and check out our user ID route.

14. We return to the same user route and enter, for example, 21 as the route parameter, and the value of 21 is present in the response, as shown in the following figure:

FIGURE 3.27 User with id 21.

Therefore, with this exercise, the main idea that we want to convey is that we should use Controller to structure our code better.

If you see the **route.swift** file, as shown in the following figure, you will notice that it is now almost empty.

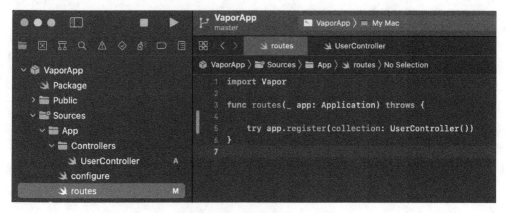

FIGURE 3.28 Route file.

The route file is simply delegating all the routes to the **UserController** or any other controller we have. Furthermore, the Controller itself is going to be dictating what kind of routes will be built and what to display on each of these routes, as shown in the following figure:

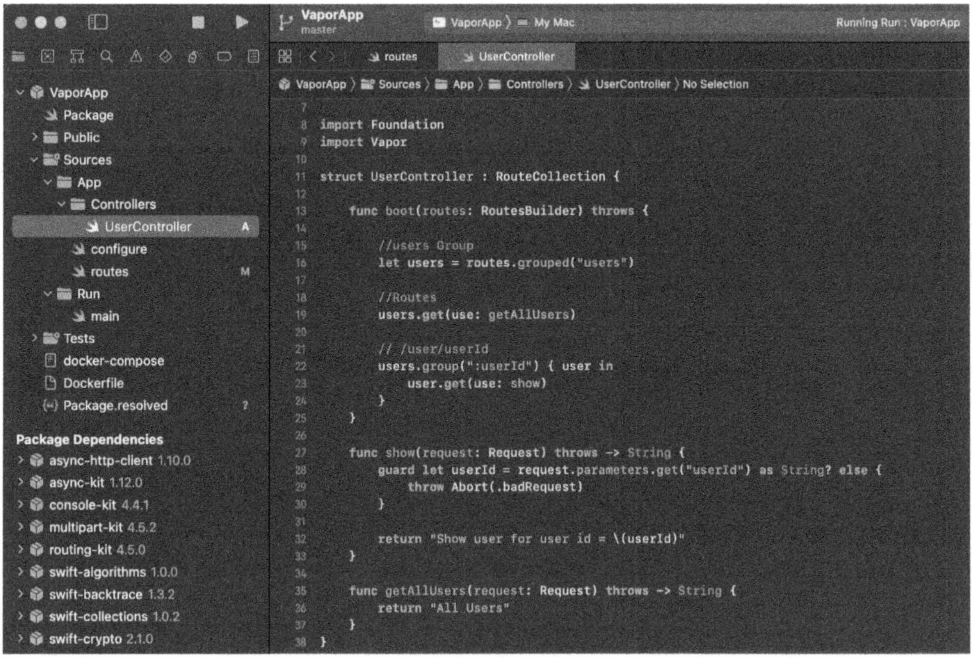

FIGURE 3.29 Controller.

Later on, we will also see how the Controller can use a repository or a model to fetch the information from a database and then return some sort of page API, and so on.

However, by all means, start using the controllers because, as is evident, they are really useful when you are structuring your application, and they will be very beneficial in the long run when you enter the maintenance phase of your code.

WORKING WITH JSON

So far, we have learned how we can return a string as a response from our route. However, in actual iPhone applications, you do want to return some sort of structured data.

If we want to return usernames in the **getAllUsers** API mentioned previously, we can go ahead and modify the API to return an array of dictionaries with key as **name** and value as username.

The new function would be something like the following:

```
func getAllUsers(request: Request) throws -> [[String:String]] {
    return [["name":"User1"], ["name":"User2"]]

}
```

1. Re-run the code again, and in the browser, type the address at **http://localhost:8080/users** to test the API. This should return an array of user dictionaries on the browser, as shown in the following figure:

FIGURE 3.30 List of users.

2. What if we also want each dictionary to have the age of the user? Let us go ahead and put the age as shown in the following:

```
func getAllUsers(request: Request) throws -> [[String:String]] {
    return [["name":"User1", "age":32], ["name":"User2", "age":56]]

}
```

3. The key is **age** and the value is an **integer**; the compiler will start giving errors because it can only return dictionaries having a **String** type value, but the **age** value is an integer. Therefore, what should we do?

Can we assume that the dictionary value will be of type **Any**? **Any** does not really conform to codable/decodable.

Therefore, the JSON format comes to our aid. Because this format is text-only, JSON data can easily be sent between computers and used by any programming language. How can we return JSON data from our Vapor API?

First of all, instead of returning an array of dictionaries, we will return a **Response** from the function. Therefore, we can return anything that is codable. Hence, we will use **JSONSerialization** to convert the user array into JSON format. Create a **Response** from JSON data and then return the response shown as follows:

```
func getAllUsers(request: Request) throws -> Response {

let users = [["name":"User1", "age":32], ["name":"User2", "age":56]]

    let data = try JSONSerialization.data(withJSONObject: users,
        options: .prettyPrinted)

    return Response(status: .ok, body: Response.Body(data: data))

}
```

Re-run the code again, and in the browser, type the address at **http://localhost:8080/users** to test the API. This should return JSON for user data on the browser, as shown in the following figure:

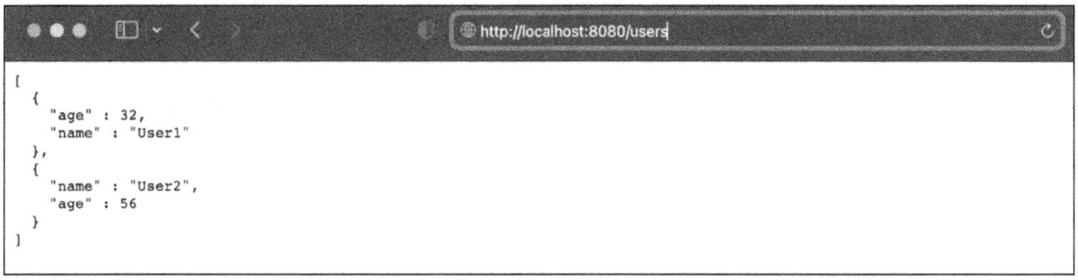

FIGURE 3.31 List of users JSON 1.

This is not a very nice approach to converting user data to JSON, as we are storing data in dictionaries. The Vapor framework does provide some protocols that can be used to easily pass around and convert the actual object into JSON. The first thing we are going to do is create a structure for the user, like the following:

```
struct User : Content{
    let name : String
    let age : Int

}
```

As is evident, the **User** conforms to the **Content**. According to the definition of content, we see that it is a protocol conforming to **Codable**, **RequestDecodable**, **ResponseEncodable**, **AsyncRequestDecodable**, and **AsyncResponseEncodable**, as shown in the following figure:

```
19  public protocol Content: Codable, RequestDecodable, ResponseEncodable, AsyncRequestDecodable,
        AsyncResponseEncodable {
20      ///  The default `MediaType` to use when _encoding_ content. This can always be overridden at the encode call.
21      ///
22      /// Default implementation is `MediaType.json` for all types.
23      ///
24      ///      struct Hello: Content {
25      ///          static let defaultContentType = .urlEncodedForm
26      ///          let message = "Hello!"
27      ///      }
28      ///
29      ///      router.get("greeting") { req in
30      ///          return Hello() // message=Hello!
31      ///      }
32      ///
33      ///      router.get("greeting2") { req in
34      ///          let res = req.response()
35      ///          try res.content.encode(Hello(), as: .json)
36      ///          return res // {"message":"Hello!"}
37      ///      }
```

FIGURE 3.32 Content.

Let us modify our **getAllUsers** function to use this struct as follows:

```
func getAllUsers(request: Request) throws -> [User] {

let users = [User(name: "User1", age: 32), User(name: "User2", age: 32)]

return users

}
```

Re-run the code again, and in the browser, type the address at **http://localhost:8080/users** to test the API. This should return JSON for user data on the browser, as shown in the following figure:

FIGURE 3.33 List of users JSON 2.

This is all good, but what if we have a complex object structure? We can assume that the user will have an address, and to capture the user address, we will create another struct as follows:

```
struct Address : Content{
    let street : String
```

```
    let state : String
    let zip : String

}
```

Furthermore, let us add a new property **address** in the **User** structure as follows:

```
struct User : Content{
    let name : String
    let age : Int
    let address : Address

}
```

Returning to the **getAllUsers** function, we must update the initializer for the **User** object:

```
func getAllUsers(request: Request) throws -> [User] {

    let address = Address(street: "Road 8 Rohini sec 8" , state:
    "Delhi", zip: "110085")

    let users = [User(name: "User1", age: 32, address: address)]
    return users

}
```

Re-run the code again, and in the browser, type the address at **http://localhost:8080/users** to test the API. This should return JSON for user data on the browser, as shown in the following figure:

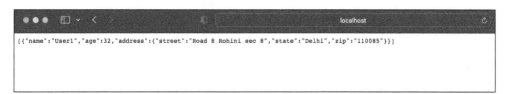

FIGURE 3.34 List of users JSON 3.

Posting JSON and Postman App

We have examined the get routes and how we can return JSON using a get request. What about the **POST** requests? Let us go ahead and see how we can implement a post request that will accept JSON. Our route is going to get the JSON decoded and return to status.

In the **UserController**, create a new function, for example, **createUser**, which will be used by a **POST** route.

```
func createUser(request: Request) throws -> HTTPStatus {
    let user = try request.content.decode(request.content)
    print(user)

    return .ok

}
```

Next, in the **boot** function, create a **POST** route for creating users.

```
//POST

users.post("create", use: createUser)
```

Re-run the code again to test our **POST** API.

All is well so far, but how do we test this API? For **GET** requests, we simply hit the routes in the browser, but in the case of **POST** requests, we need to send a **POST** body with user data to create a new user.

Postman.app comes to the rescue. You can download the **Postman.app** for macOS from (*https://www.postman.com/downloads/*).

After downloading and installing, launch the app, and you will arrive at the window, as shown in the following figure:

FIGURE 3.35 Postman.

Click on the dropdown at left and select **POST**, as shown by the red circled area in the following figure. Furthermore, in the URL field, type the URL for the create route as `http://localhost:8080/users/create`, as shown by the box area in the following figure:

FIGURE 3.36 POST Request 1.

As this is a **POST** request, we will have to provide a request body for the content to which we will pass our JSON. For that, click on **Body** and on the **raw** link in the Postman window, as shown by the two circled areas in the following figure:

FIGURE 3.37 POST Request 2.

Proceed to the **Header** section left of the **Body** link, and under the **KEY** column, type **Content-Type**, as shown in the following figure:

FIGURE 3.38 POST Request 3.

After selecting the key, in the **VALUE** column, type **application/json**, as shown in the following figure to specify the content type attached to the body of the **POST** request:

FIGURE 3.39 POST Request 4.

It is time to provide the user object as JSON in the body of the **POST** request. Go back to the **Body** section, as shown in the following figure, and type your JSON in the text area, as shown in the following:

```
{

    "name":"New User",
    "age":32,
```

```
    "address": {

        "street":"Road 8 Rohini sec 8",
        "state":"Delhi",

    }

}
```

We have provided the wrong JSON syntax, for which Postman's editor will highlight the error with a ~ as shown in the figure, and also, if you look closely, we have not provided a `zip code` in the JSON.

Now run the code, and when the service is up and running, press the **Send** button to execute the **POST** request. In the response section, you will see a failure response with status code **400 Bad Request** and an error response as follows:

```
{

    "error": true,

    "reason": "Value required for key 'address.zip'."

}
```

Refer to the following figure:

FIGURE 3.40 POST Request 5.

Let us correct our JSON structure and provide the following JSON to the **POST** request:

```
{

    "name":"New User",
    "age":32,
    "address": {

        "street":"Road 8 Rohini sec 8",
        "state":"Delhi",
        "zip" : "110085"

    }

}
```

Furthermore, press the **Send** button and execute the **POST** request. This time, the service will respond with status **200 OK** and response **1**; see the following figure:

FIGURE 3.41 POST Request 6.

CONCLUSION

To recap, we covered Routes and Controllers in Vapor and also covered working with JSON and Postman for **GET** and **POST** requests. With this chapter, we have laid the groundwork for our journey in the domain of full-stack development on iOS.

In the next chapter, we will examine concepts pertaining to async, logging, error handling, and Leaf.

4

ASYNC AND HTML RENDERING IN VAPOR

INTRODUCTION

In this chapter, we will continue to understand the other base concepts of Vapor in continuation of *Chapter 3: Routing, MVC, and JSON in Vapor*.

STRUCTURE

In this chapter, we will cover the following topics:

- Async
- Logging
- Environment
- Errors
- Stack traces
- Leaf

OBJECTIVES

In continuation of the previous chapter, this chapter aims to extend the basic understanding of async, logging, capturing errors and stack traces, and finally, handling HTML rendering in a Vapor project. In this chapter, we will implement a small part of the code to showcase HTML rendering on a Web page using Leaf and Vapor routes.

ASYNC

Asynchronous programming is an essential part of developing scalable Web applications. With Vapor, developers can leverage Swift's native concurrency features to write asynchronous code that efficiently handles multiple concurrent requests. In Vapor, asynchronous programming is typically achieved using the async and await keywords, which allow developers to write non-blocking code that can handle I/O-intensive operations, such as network requests and database queries, without blocking the main thread. This makes it possible to handle numerous requests concurrently, improving the performance and scalability of the Web application.

Async Await

Swift 5.5 introduced concurrency to the language with async/await. This provided a highly efficient way of handling asynchronous code in Swift and Vapor applications.

As discussed before, Vapor is built on top of SwiftNIO, which provides primitive types for low-level asynchronous programming, and these were centrally staged throughout, even before async/await arrived. With Swift 5.5, it is recommended to use async/await instead of **EventLoopFutures** to simplify the code and make it much easier to read and debug.

Vapor's APIs now offer both **EventLoopFuture** and async/await versions. As a best practice, you should only use one programming model per route handler and not the mix and match of both approaches.

Migrating to Async/Await

There are a few steps we need to take to migrate to Async/Await. To start with, you must be on macOS 12 Monterey or greater and should have Xcode 13.1 or greater. For other platforms, we may use Swift 5.5 or greater running on that platform.

In **Package.swift**, set the tools version to 5.5 at the top of the file, set the platform version to macOS 12, and update the run target to mark it as an executable target, as shown in the following figure:

```
∨ 🌐 VaporApp                          🌐 VaporApp ⟩ 🧩 Package ⟩ No Selection
    🧩 Package                         1  // swift-tools-version:5.6
  > 📁 Public                          2  import PackageDescription
  > 📁 Sources                         3
  > 📁 Tests                           4  let package = Package(
    🗋 docker-compose                  5      name: "VaporApp",
    🗋 Dockerfile                      6      platforms: [
    (~) Package.resolved          7    7          .macOS(.v12)
                                       8      ],
Package Dependencies                   9      dependencies: [
  > 🌐 async-http-client 1.10.0       10          // 🔷 A server-side Swift web framework.
  > 🌐 async-kit 1.12.0               11          .package(url: "https://github.com/vapor/vapor.git", from: "4.0.0"),
  > 🌐 console-kit 4.4.1              12      ],
  > 🌐 multipart-kit 4.5.2            13      targets: [
  > 🌐 routing-kit 4.5.0              14          .target(
  > 🌐 swift-algorithms 1.0.0         15              name: "App",
  > 🌐 swift-backtrace 1.3.2          16              dependencies: [
  > 🌐 swift-collections 1.0.2        17                  .product(name: "Vapor", package: "vapor")
  > 🌐 swift-crypto 2.1.0             18              ],
  > 🌐 swift-log 1.4.2                19              swiftSettings: [
  > 🌐 swift-metrics 2.3.1            20                  // Enable better optimizations when building in Release configuration. Despite the use of
  > 🌐 swift-nio 2.40.0               21                  // the .unsafeFlags construct required by SwiftPM, this flag is recommended for Release
  > 🌐 swift-nio-extras 1.12.0        22                  // builds. See
  > 🌐 swift-nio-http2 1.22.0                            //  <https://github.com/swift-server/guides/blob/main/docs/building
  > 🌐 swift-nio-ssl 2.20.0                              //  .md#building-for-production> for details.
  > 🌐 swift-nio-transport-services 1.1...  23           .unsafeFlags(["-cross-module-optimization"], .when(configuration: .release))
  > 🌐 swift-numerics 1.0.2           24              ]
  > 🌐 vapor 4.61.1                   25          ),
                                      26          .executableTarget(name: "Run", dependencies: [.target(name: "App")]),
                                      27          .testTarget(name: "AppTests", dependencies: [
                                      28              .target(name: "App"),
                                      29              .product(name: "XCTVapor", package: "vapor"),
                                      30          ])
                                      31      ]
                                      32  )
```

FIGURE 4.1 Set tool versions.

LOGGING

Vapor's logging API uses SwiftLog (*https://github.com/apple/swift-log*) underneath, which makes it compatible with all of SwiftLog's backend implementations (*https://github.com/apple/swift-log#backends*).

Vapor provides a few easy ways to use instances of **Logger** for outputting log messages. Each incoming **Request** has a unique logger associated with it that we should use for any logs specific to that request, as shown as follows:

```
app.get("hello") { req -> String in

    req.logger.info("Hello, logs!")

    return "Hello, world!"

}
```

The request logger includes a unique UUID identifying the incoming request to make tracking logs easier.

For log messages during app boot and configuration, use the following application's logger:

```
app.logger.info("Setting up migrations...")
```

There could be situations where we do not have access to the **Application** or the **Request**. In such cases, we can initialize a new custom **Logger**:

```
let logger = Logger(label: "dev.logger.myAppLogs")

logger.info("some info log")
```

While custom loggers still output to the configured logging backend, they lack important metadata attached, like the request UUID. Hence, it is advisable to use request- or application-specific loggers wherever possible.

SwiftLog also supports several different logging levels:

TABLE 4.1 SwiftLog logging levels.

Log-level	Description
trace	This log level should be used for messages that contain information for tracing the execution of a program.
debug	This log level should be for messages that contain information for the purpose of debugging a program.
info	This log level should be used for informational messages.
notice	This log level should be used for conditions that are not error conditions but that may require special attention and handling.
warning	This log level should be used for messages that are not error conditions but more severe than notice.
Error	This log level should be used for error conditions.
critical	This log level should be used for critical error conditions that require immediate attention.

When a critical message is logged, the logging backend can perform more heavy-weight operations to capture the system state and facilitate debugging. By default, Vapor will use the info level for logging. When running in the production environment, notice levels will be used to improve performance.

Regardless of the default environment mode, we can override the logging level as per the need of our application to increase or decrease the number of logs produced.

One way is to pass the optional **--log** flag while booting our application:

```
vapor run serve --log debug
```

Another way is to set the **LOG_LEVEL** environment variable:

```
export LOG_LEVEL=debug

vapor run serve
```

SwiftLog is configured by bootstrapping the **LoggingSystem** once per process, and this is typically done in **main.swift**:

```
import Vapor

var env = try Environment.detect()

try LoggingSystem.bootstrap(from: &env)
```

The **bootstrap(from:)** is a helper method that will configure the default log handler based on command-line arguments and environment variables. The default log handler can output messages to the terminal.

However, that is not all. We can override Vapor's default log handler and register our own, like the following:

```
import Logging LoggingSystem.bootstrap { label in

    StreamLogHandler.standardOutput(label: label)

}
```

All of SwiftLog's supported backends will work with Vapor. However, changing the log level using command-line arguments and environment variables is only possible with Vapor's default log handler.

ENVIRONMENT

Vapor's Environment API helps us configure our app dynamically. By default, the app will use the development environment. We can define other useful environments, like production or staging, and change how the app is configured in each case. We can also load the variables from the process's environment or **.env** files, depending on the app's needs.

We can access the current environment using **app.environment**. We can switch this property in configure **(_:)** to execute different configuration logic:

```
switch app.environment {

case .production:
```

```
    app.databases.use(.   )

default:

    app.databases.use(.   )

}
```

By default, the app runs in the development environment. This can be changed by passing the --env (**-e**) flag during **app** boot:

```
vapor run serve --env production
```

The following environments are included in Vapor:

Name	Short name	Description
production	prod	Deployed to end users.
development	dev	Local development.
testing	test	Unit testing.

We can pass either the full or short name to the **--env** (**-e**) flag, like the following:

```
vapor run serve -e prod
```

ERRORS

Vapor builds upon Swift's **Error** protocol for handling errors. Route handlers in Vapor can either throw an error or return a failed **EventLoopFuture**. Throwing or returning a Swift Error will result in a status response of 500, and the error will be logged. **AbortError** and **DebuggableError** are used to change the resulting response and logging, respectively. **ErrorMiddleware** handles the errors. ErrorMiddleware is added to the application by default and can be replaced with custom logic if desired.

Abort

Vapor provides a default error struct **Abort**. **Abor** conforms to both **AbortError** and **DebuggableError**. We can initialize this with an HTTP status and optional failure reason as follows:

```
// 404 status code, default "Not Found" reason used.

throw Abort(.notFound)
```

```
// 401 status code, customized reason used.

throw Abort(.unauthorized, reason: "Invalid Credentials")
```

In old asynchronous architecture, where throwing was not supported, the method must return an **EventLoopFuture**; like in a **flatMap** closure, we can return a failed future:

```
guard let user = user else {

    req.eventLoop.makeFailedFuture(Abort(.notFound))

}

return user.save()
```

Vapor provides a helper extension for unwrapping futures with optional values:

unwrap(or:):

```
User.find(id, on: db)

    .unwrap(or: Abort(.notFound))

    .flatMap

{ user in

    // Non-optional User supplied to closure.

}
```

In the case of **User.find** returning nil, the future will fail with the supplied error. Otherwise, the **flatMap** will be supplied with a non-optional value. If we are using **async/await**, then we can handle optional as follows:

```
guard let user = try await User.find(id, on: db) {

    throw Abort(.notFound)

}
```

Abort Error

By default, any Swift Error thrown by a route closure will result in a **500 Internal Server Error** response. While running the program in debug mode, **ErrorMiddleware** includes a description of the error, which is stripped out when the project is built in release mode for security reasons.

To configure the reason or HTTP response status for a particular error, it should conform to **AbortError**:

```
import Vapor

enum CustomUserError {

    case userNotLoggedIn

    case invalidEmail(String)

}


extension CustomUserError: AbortError {

    var reason: String {

        switch self {

        case .userNotLoggedIn:

            return "User not logged in."

        case .invalidEmail(let email):

            return "Email address not valid: \(email)."

        }

    }


    var status: HTTPStatus {

        switch self {

        case .userNotLoggedIn:

            return .unauthorized

        case .invalidEmail:

            return .badRequest

        }

    }

}
```

Debuggable Error

When routes throw errors, **ErrorMiddleware** uses the **Logger. report(error:)** method for logging errors. This method checks the conformance to protocols such as **CustomStringConvertible** and **LocalizedError** for logging readable messages.

For customized error logging, we need to conform errors to **DebuggableError**. This protocol includes properties such as a unique identifier, source location, and stack trace. Most of these properties are optional to make adopting conformance easy.

The custom error conforming to the **DebuggableError** should be a struct so that it can store source and stack trace information if needed. The following is an example of the **CustomUserError** enum updated to use a struct and capture error source information:

```
import Vapor


struct CustomUserError: DebuggableError {

    enum Value {

        case userNotLoggedIn

        case invalidEmail(String)

    }


    var identifier: String {

        switch self.value {

        case .userNotLoggedIn:

            return "userNotLoggedIn"

        case .invalidEmail:

            return "invalidEmail"

        }

    }
```

```swift
var reason: String {

    switch self.value {

    case .userNotLoggedIn:

        return "User not logged in."

    case .invalidEmail(let email):

        return "Email address not valid: \(email)."

    }

}


var value: Value

var source: ErrorSource?


init(

    _ value: Value,

    file: String = #file,

    function: String = #function,

    line: UInt = #line,

    column: UInt = #column

) {

    self.value = value

    self.source = .init(

        file: file,

        function: function,

        line: line,

        column: column

    )

}

}
```

STACK TRACES

In Swift Vapor, stack traces provide a detailed report of what went wrong in your code, making it easier to identify and fix errors. Stack traces can be generated for unhandled errors and exceptions, and they can be configured to include various levels of detail, depending on your needs.

When an error occurs, Vapor generates a stack trace that includes information such as the file and line number where the error occurred, the function that was executing at the time of the error, and the call stack leading up to the error. This information is presented in a clear and easy-to-read format, making it easier to identify the source of the problem.

By default, stack traces in Vapor include detailed information, such as the values of variables and arguments at each step of the call stack. This level of detail can be very helpful when debugging complex issues, but it can also make stack traces very long and difficult to read. For this reason, Vapor provides a number of configuration options that allow you to customize the level of detail included in stack traces.

Overall, stack traces in Swift Vapor provide an essential tool for debugging your code and improving the reliability of your applications. By providing detailed information about errors and exceptions, stack traces help you quickly identify and fix issues in your code, ensuring that your applications are always running smoothly. Vapor supports viewing stack traces for both normal Swift errors and crashes.

Swift Backtrace

Vapor uses the **SwiftBacktrace** library to provide stack traces after a fatal error or assertion. For using **SwiftBacktrace**, the app must include debug symbols during compilation:

```
swift build -c release -Xswiftc -g
```

Error Traces

By default, **Abort** captures the current stack trace when initialized. To achieve this with custom error types, they need to conform to **DebuggableError** and store **StackTrace.capture()**.

```
import Vapor
```

```
struct CustomUserError: DebuggableError {

    var identifier: String

    var reason: String

    var stackTrace: StackTrace?


    init(
        identifier: String,
        reason: String,
        stackTrace: StackTrace? = .capture()
    ) {
        self.identifier = identifier
        self.reason = reason
        self.stackTrace = stackTrace
    }

}
```

When the application's log level is set to debug or lower, error stack traces will be included in the log output. Stack traces are not captured when the log level is greater than .debug. This behavior can be overridden by setting **StackTrace.isCaptureEnabled** manually in configure.

```
// Capture stack traces regardless of log level.
StackTrace.isCaptureEnabled = true
```

ErrorMiddleware

ErrorMiddleware is added to the application by default. **ErrorMiddleware** converts Swift errors that have been thrown by the route handlers into HTTP responses. Without **ErrorMiddleware**, errors thrown will result in the connection being closed without a response.

To customize error handling beyond **AbortError** and **DebuggableError**, we can replace **ErrorMiddleware** with our own error-handling logic. To achieve this, first, we need to remove the default error middleware by setting

app.middleware to an empty configuration. Then, add custom error handling middleware as the first middleware to the application.

```
// Remove all existing middleware.

app.middleware = .init()

// Add custom error handling middleware first.

app.middleware.use(MyErrorMiddleware())
```

LEAF

What exactly are Leaf templates? Consider that we have a page that consists of a header and footer. However, on Web pages, we also have content, and we are going to represent content with data. This content is getting there from the server, as the server is responsible for getting the content, probably from the database, and somehow putting it on the page.

How does the server put the content on the page? At this point, Leaf comes to help us. Leaf is a powerful templating language with Swift-inspired syntax. We can use it to generate dynamic HTML pages for a front-end Web site.

For using Leaf in the project, the first step is to add it as a dependency to the project in the SPM package manifest file. Navigate to the **Package.swift** file and add the Leaf dependency.

```
dependencies: [

    //Other dependencies.......

    .package(url: "https://github.com/vapor/vapor.git", from: "4.0.0"),

]
```

Furthermore, add dependency to the target as well:

```
targets: [

    .target(

        name: "App",

        dependencies: [

            .product(name: "Vapor", package: "vapor"),

            .product(name: "Leaf", package: "leaf")],
```

After this **Package.swift** file will look as shown in the following figure:

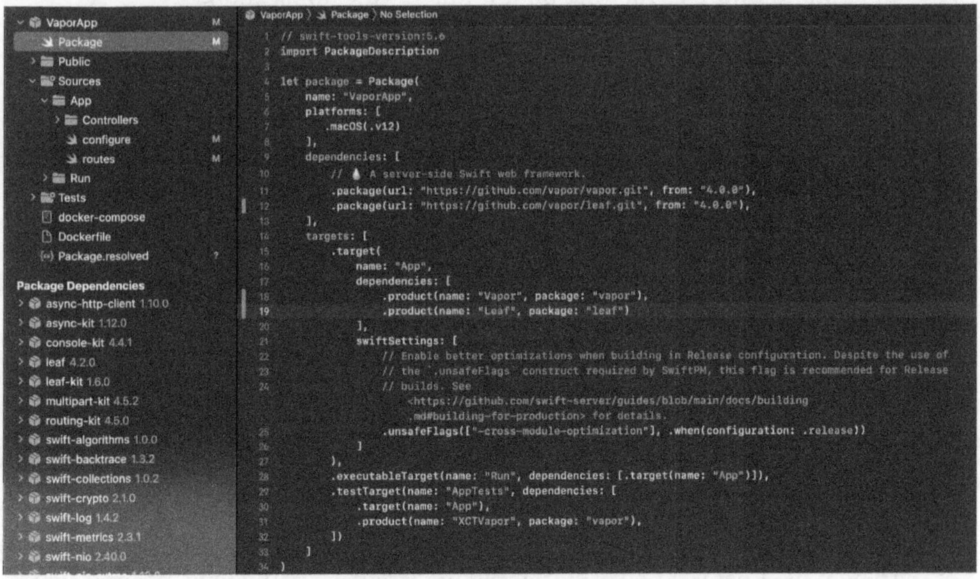

FIGURE 4.2 Add Leaf dependency.

Now in **Configure.swift**, configure Vapor to use it as follows:

```
import Leaf

app.views.use(.leaf)
```

After this, the **Configure.swift** file will look as shown in the following figure:

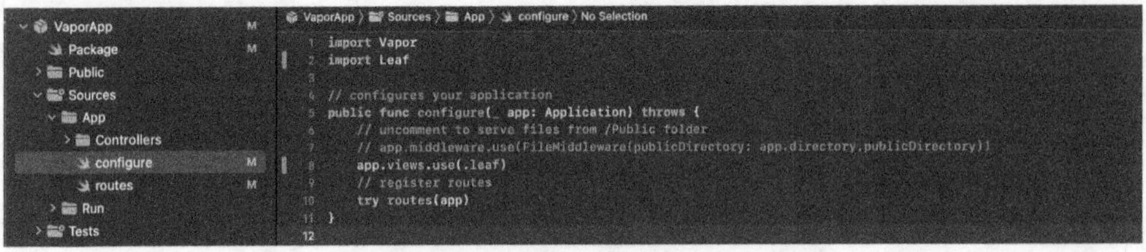

FIGURE 4.3 Configure Leaf dependency.

The next thing would be for us to create or render a page using Leaf templates. By default, when we are using Vapor, it is going to be looking for Leaf pages inside a directory called **Resources**. This directory has to be on the project level; therefore, we can go ahead and add a new folder. That folder should be named **Resources**.

Let us go ahead and add a folder named **Resources**, as shown in the following figure:

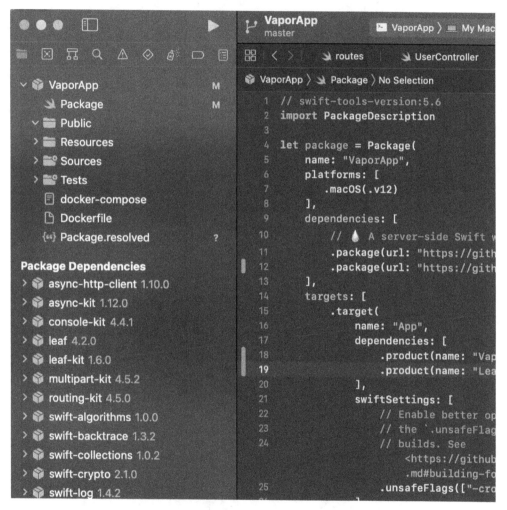

FIGURE 4.4 Leaf Resources.

Inside the **Resources** folder, we will have to create another folder called **Views**, as shown in the following figure. All the views that we are going to be creating will be living inside this folder:

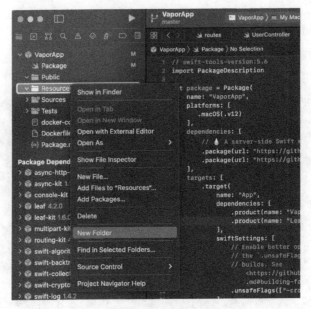

FIGURE 4.5 Leaf Views.

After this, we will add a new file to the **Views** folder, as shown in the following figure:

FIGURE 4.6 View File.

This is going to be a Swift file, as shown in the following figure:

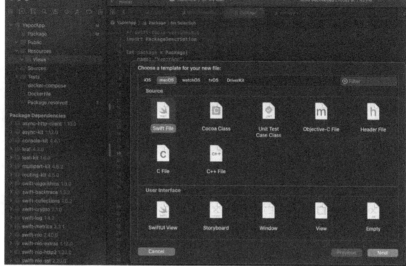

FIGURE 4.7 View File 1.

Once the file is added, rename it to **index.leaf**. The extension we will use is Leaf because it is a Leaf template file. In this file, we are going to be writing our HTML code. We can start with a very simple template shown as follows:

```
<html>

    <h1>Hello Vapor Leaf!!</h1>

</html>
```

At the end, the **index.html** file will look as shown in the following figure:

FIGURE 4.8 Index File.

Subsequently, we must navigate to our routes and confirm that we are rendering the file based on an appropriate route. Therefore, proceed to the route file and create a route for rendering the new Leaf file, as shown in the following figure:

FIGURE 4.9 Route.

It is time to run the project and test the HTML rendering through Leaf. Press the **Play** button to run the project and wait for the following message in the console.

```
[ NOTICE ] Server starting at http://127.0.0.1:8080
```

Open the browser, and in the address bar, type **http://localhost:8080** and press *Enter*. You should see the HTML message in the browser, as shown in the following figure:

FIGURE 4.10 HTML Rendering.

While this is all good, it is still a static HTML page. Let us dive a bit deeper to render a dynamic HTML page. First, let us create a struct **Movies** with properties such as name and year of release that will conform to the **Content** protocol.

```
struct Movies: Content {

    let name: String

    let releaseYear: String

}
```

NOTE *For the sake of simplicity in this example, this struct was created in routes. swift, but as a practical example, this should be in a separate controller.*

Now go back to **index.html** and modify the HTML to expect properties from this struct dynamically. Using the following HTML template, we should now be able to pass **Movie** information to the HTML page dynamically through our route:

```
<html>

    <h1>Hello Vapor Leaf!!</h1>

    <h2>Movie #(name) released in #(releaseYear)</h2>

</html>
```

Let us update the renderer function in the routes shown as follows:

```
app.get { req -> EventLoopFuture<View> in

    req.view.render("index", Movies(name: "Harry Potter and the
Philosopher's Stone", releaseYear: "2001"))

}
```

Run the project by pressing the **Play** button again and refreshing the page with the address **http://localhost:8080**. You should see a page as shown in the following figure:

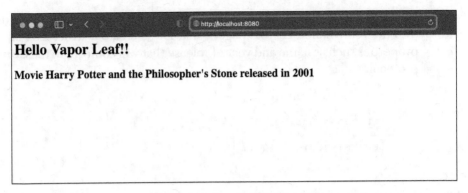

FIGURE 4.11 Dynamic HTML Rendering.

We will limit discussion on Leaf here, as we will not use Leaf with the iOS frontend. However, if you want to create a Web-based project, it is highly recommended to go deep with Leaf implementation.

CONCLUSION

To recap, we have covered async, error handling, logging, stack traces, and HTML rendering using Leaf and routes in this chapter. While we will not use Leaf in our final project with the iOS frontend, this was a much-needed topic to understand the workflows and internals of Swift Vapor in continuation with *Chapter 3: Routing, MVC, and JSON in Vapor.*

In the next chapter, we will explore data management basics with Fluent on the Vapor side and Core Data on the iOS side.

POSTGRESQL INTEGRATION IN VAPOR

INTRODUCTION

While APIs are what we need to establish communication between client and server, there is always a need to store and persist data in some database. Databases provide reliable and persistent storage and performant retrieval of data. In the absence of any persistent data store, applications will have to store information in memory, which will be lost once we stop the application. As a best practice, we should decouple storage from the application to allow it to scale across multiple application instances, all backed by the same database.

In this chapter, we will explore database operations, ORMs, and data modeling techniques available with Vapor.

STRUCTURE

In this chapter, we will discuss the following topics:

- Data persistence with Vapor
- Installing and setting up PostgreSQL
- Fluent ORM
- CRUD operations
- Migrations

- Postico
- Create and save model

OBJECTIVES

In this chapter, we will study the integration of PostgreSQL with Vapor. PostgreSQL is an open-source, relational database system that focuses on extensibility and standards. It is designed for enterprise use and also has native support for geometric primitives, such as coordinates, which comes in handy when working with Fluent, which also supports these primitives and saves nested types, such as dictionaries, directly into PostgreSQL.

DATA PERSISTENCE WITH VAPOR

Vapor supports Swift-native drivers for the following databases:

Relational databases:

- SQLite
- MySQL
- PostgreSQL

Non-relational databases:

- MongoDB

Relational databases store their data in structured tables with defined schema, and hence, these are efficient at storing and querying structured data. While relational databases are good for defined structures, it is cumbersome to change the data structure. Non-relational databases, on the other hand, can store large amounts of unstructured data.

For the scope of this chapter, we will use a relational database, PostgreSQL, which is an open-source relational database. It is designed for enterprise use and also comes in handy when working with Fluent.

INSTALLING AND SETTING UP POSTGRESQL

In this section, we will integrate our Vapor server-side application with the PostgreSQL database.

1. Open the browser and open the Web site at *https://www.postgresql.org*.

2. Click on the **Download** link as shown in the following figure:

FIGURE 5.1 PostgreSQL.org.

3. As shown in the following figure, PostgreSQL is available on multiple platforms. As we are working on macOS, we will select the **macOS** platform on the page:

FIGURE 5.2 PostgreSQL install options.

4. As we arrive at the next page, we will see multiple **macOS packages** on the page. The easiest of these options would be to install **Postgres. app**, as shown in the following figure:

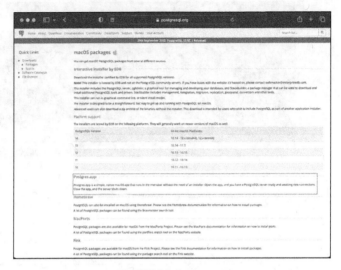

FIGURE 5.3 Postgres.app.

5. Click on the **Postgres.app** link to arrive at the **Introduction** page, as shown in the following figure:

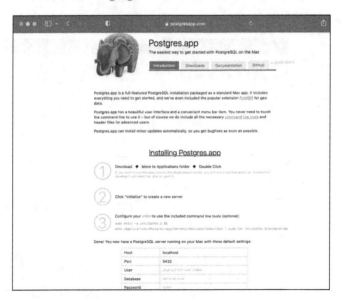

FIGURE 5.4 Postgres.app introduction page.

6. Navigate to the **Downloads** tab and download the **Latest Release**, as shown in the following figure:

FIGURE 5.5 Postgres.app downloads.

7. After downloading, open the dmg file and install the app in the **Application** folder. Launch the app. After launch, you will see an **App Window** and a status menu in the top menu bar, as shown in the following figure:

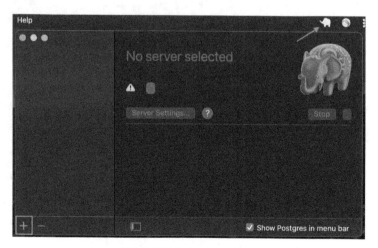

FIGURE 5.6 Postgres.app launch.

8. Click on the **+** button shown in *Figure 5.6* and enter server details to create a PostgreSQL server, as shown in the following figure:

FIGURE 5.7 Creating a PostgreSQL server.

9. Once the server is created, we can start the server using the **Start** button, as shown in the following figure:

FIGURE 5.8 Start the PostgreSQL server.

10. As soon as you start the PostgreSQL server, you will see a few default databases already available, as shown in the following figure:

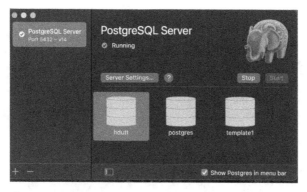

FIGURE 5.9 PostgreSQL server databases.

11. Double-click on the default database created by your username, in this case, **hdutt**. This will prompt you with a system alert, as shown in the following figure. Press **OK**.

FIGURE 5.10 PostgreSQL system alert.

12. Pressing **OK** on the alert will launch a terminal, as shown in the following figure:

```
● ● ●                    hdutt — psql -p5432 hdutt — 80×24
Last login: Sat Oct  1 21:15:30 on ttys000
hdutt@HDUTT-M-40QV ~ % /Applications/Postgres.app/Contents/Versions/14/bin/psql
-p5432 "hdutt"
psql (14.5)
Type "help" for help.

hdutt=# □
```

FIGURE 5.11 PostgreSQL terminal.

This terminal is very important because it is actually the PostgreSQL terminal through which we can interact with PostgreSQL.

13. As shown in *Figure 5.11*, we are connected to the **hdutt** database. If we do not want to use this default database, we can create a brand-new database, and for that, we can go ahead and run the command **CREATE** database and then the name of the database as shown in the following figure:

```
● ● ●                    hdutt — psql -p5432 hdutt — 80×24
Last login: Sat Oct  1 21:15:30 on ttys000
hdutt@HDUTT-M-40QV ~ % /Applications/Postgres.app/Contents/Versions/14/bin/psql
-p5432 "hdutt"
psql (14.5)
Type "help" for help.

hdutt=# CREATE DATABASE NewPostgreDB;
```

FIGURE 5.12 Create a new database.

14. Press *Enter* after writing the **CREATE** statement, and this will print **CREATE DATABASE** in the terminal on success, as shown in the following figure:

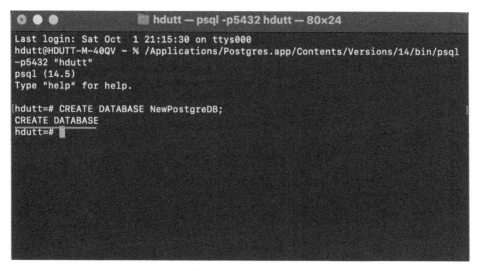

FIGURE 5.13 Database created 1.

15. We can verify the creation of this new database, **NewPostgreDB**, in the **postgres.app**, as shown in the following figure:

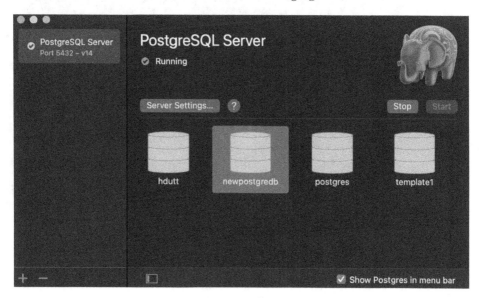

FIGURE 5.14 Database created 2.

FLUENT ORM

Fluent is an ORM framework for Swift that takes advantage of Swift's strong type system to provide an easy-to-use interface for the persistent database. Using Fluent, we can create model types that will represent data structures in the database. These models are then used to perform create, read, update, and delete operations instead of writing raw queries.

Adding Fluent to a New Project

There are two ways to add Fluent to your project. One is to add at the very inception of the project, and another is to add after project creation once you realize that your project needs ORM.

Therefore, first, let us see how we can add Fluent while creating a new project.

1. Open the terminal and execute the **cd** command, followed by the path to the desired directory.

2. Create a new Vapor project using the command **vapor new sample PostgreProject**. This will present an option to add Fluent to the project, as shown in the following figure:

```
● ● ●          Codes — vapor new samplePostgreProject — 80×24

Last login: Sun Oct  2 11:09:36 on console
[hdutt@HDUTT-M-40QV ~ % cd /Users/hdutt/Book/Book/Codes
[hdutt@HDUTT-M-40QV Codes % vapor new samplePostgreProject
Cloning template...
name: samplePostgreProject
Would you like to use Fluent? (--fluent/--no-fluent)
y/n>
```

FIGURE 5.15 Add fluent.

3. Type **y** and press *Enter* to add Fluent. This will present options for databases, as shown in the following figure:

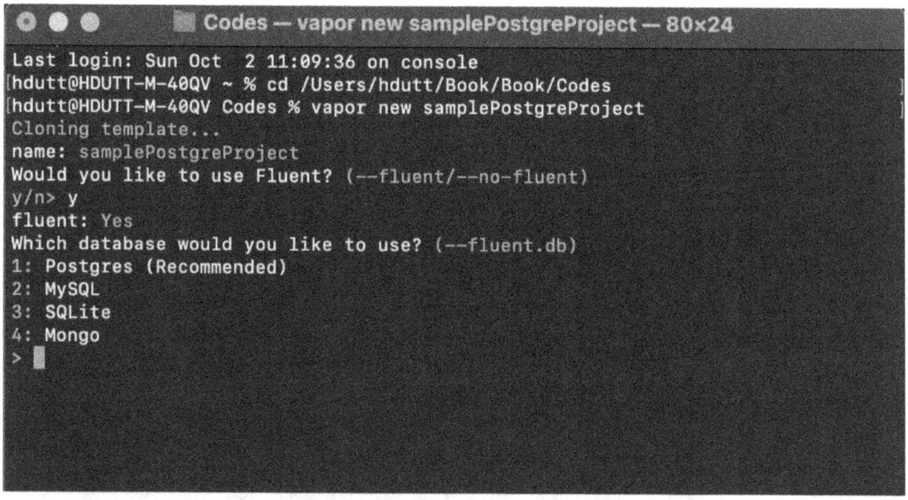

FIGURE 5.16 Add database.

4. To add PostgreSQL (Postgres), type **1** and *Enter*. This will add Postgres to your project and ask for other options, as shown in the following figure:

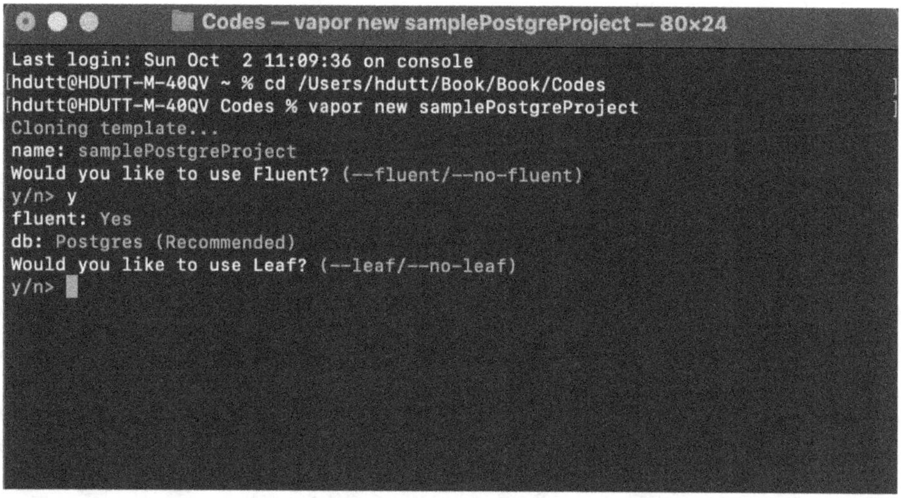

FIGURE 5.17 Postgres selected.

5. For options like Leaf and other such options, select as per project needs. We will then open the newly created project by again executing the **cd** command, followed by the path to the project directory, and typing **open Package.json**. As the project opens, you will find Fluent dependencies under the dependencies section, as shown in the following figure:

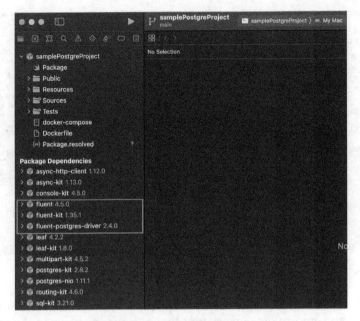

FIGURE 5.18 Fluent dependencies in the project.

6. If we open the **`Package.swift`** file, we will see an entry for Fluent under the dependencies, as shown in the following figure:

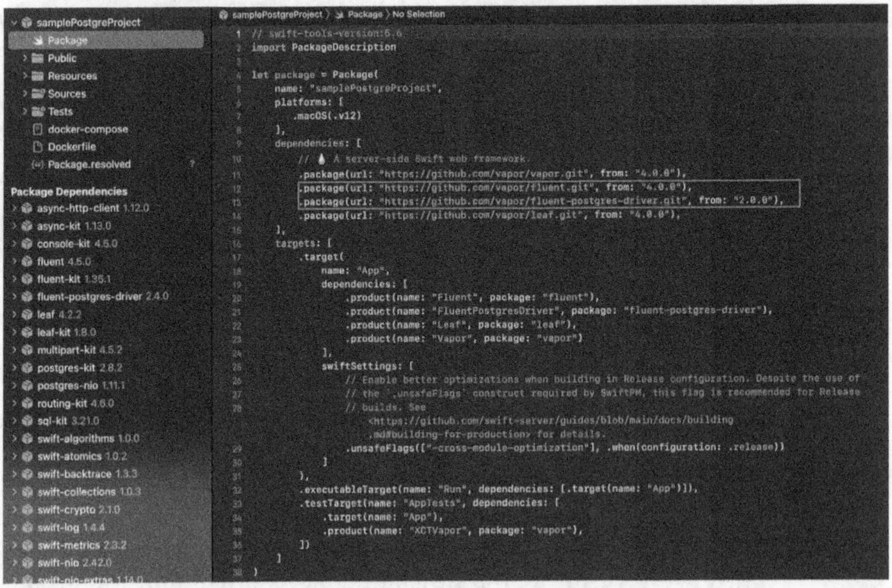

FIGURE 5.19 Fluent dependencies in Package.swift.

Adding Fluent to an Existing Project

If you do not include Fluent at the inception of the project but realize later in the project development that you need Fluent, you can easily do that. Navigate to the **Package.swift** file and include lines 12, 13, 20, and 21, as shown in *Figure 5.19*. Build the code again.

CRUD OPERATIONS

CRUD is an acronym for **Create**, **Read**, **Update**, and **Delete** operations for creating and managing persistent data elements in relational and NoSQL databases.

The first thing we need to perform CRUD operations is to create a database. In previous sections and *Figure 5.12*, we have already created a new database. In this section, we will create a new table in our database using Migration.

However, before that, open the project by running the following commands in the terminal:

```
cd path to project directory

open Packages.swift
```

If you have added Fluent at the time of the creation of the project, you will get some

boilerplate example code in the **docker-compose.yml** file and the **configure.swift** file. If you have added Fluent later in the project, you can still follow these templates to connect the project to the database.

Let us look at and understand the boilerplate code. As shown in the following figure, the boilerplate code in **docker-compose.yml** has some constants that are needed to make a connection to the database. Refer to the following figure:

NOTE *Docker Compose is a way to specify the list of different containers that work together as a single unit while using Docker containers. Using Docker Compose, we can spin up your Vapor app and a PostgreSQL database instance, which can communicate with each other but are isolated from other instances running on the same host, and that too using a single command.*

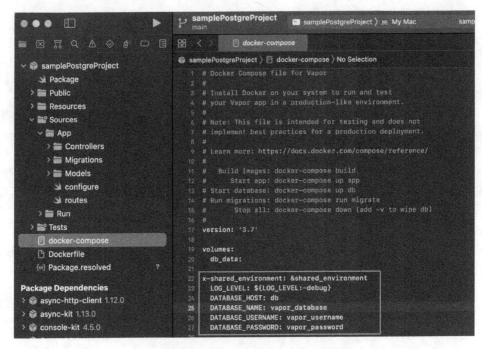

FIGURE 5.20 Boilerplate environment variable—Docker.

Let us update this boilerplate code as per the configuration we require, as shown in the following figure. In the **DATABASE_HOST**, we will put **localhost,** as our server will be running on a local host. Similarly, we can update **DATABASE_ NAME** to **newpostgredb**, which is the name of our newly created database:

FIGURE 5.21 Custom environment variable —Docker.

NOTE   *Configuration changes in docker-compose.yaml will be used only when we are working with Docker.*

Check the boilerplate code in **`configure.swift`,** as shown in the following figure:

FIGURE 5.22 Configure.swift—Boilerplate.

At this point, in *Figure 5.22* lines 1 and 2, we see that in order to create a database connection, we first need to import both **`Fluent`** and **`FluentPostgresDriver`**.

Then, in the configure function, we will write code to use our database. As we are using the **`postgres`** (PostgreSQL) database in our project, in the **`use`** function, we will pass **`.postgre`**.

At this point, if you observe, for each parameter, this code fetches values from **`Environment variable`**s defined in **`docker-compose.yaml`**, and if the value is not found in **`Environment variables`**, it is passing some default values.

As we are not using Docker as of now, **`Environment variables`** defined in **`docker-compose.yaml`** will not be available here; therefore, the default parameter values will be used. Hence, we need to update these default values to make the connection with the database, as shown in the following figure:

FIGURE 5.23 Configure.swift—Custom database configuration.

In *Figure 5.23*, line 19, you will observe that we are adding a migration named **CreateToDo**. Let us understand what Migration is and how to use it with models to save data in the database.

MIGRATIONS

Migrations are version control systems for the database. Each Migration defines a change made to the database and how to undo it. By modifying the database through migrations, we create a consistent, testable, and shareable database that can evolve over time.

In the previous section, we studied the code that allows us to connect to the **postgres** database. Our next task is to define the schema and create tables in the database. When using Fluent, it is always a good idea to write migrations for the table so that later on, we can make changes to the table schema and easily navigate through the version control problems.

NOTE   *Do not use any database editor or tool to make changes in your tables when you are using Fluent with migrations. Any changes made manually or using some tools will not be captured in migrations and will cause corruption of the database when the Migration runs.*

Let us now checkout the boilerplate code for the Migration in our sample code. Navigate to the **Migrations** folder in the project hierarchy, and there you will find **CreateTodo.swift** file. Click on the file, and we will see the boilerplate migration code for creating a table **todos**, as shown in the following figure:

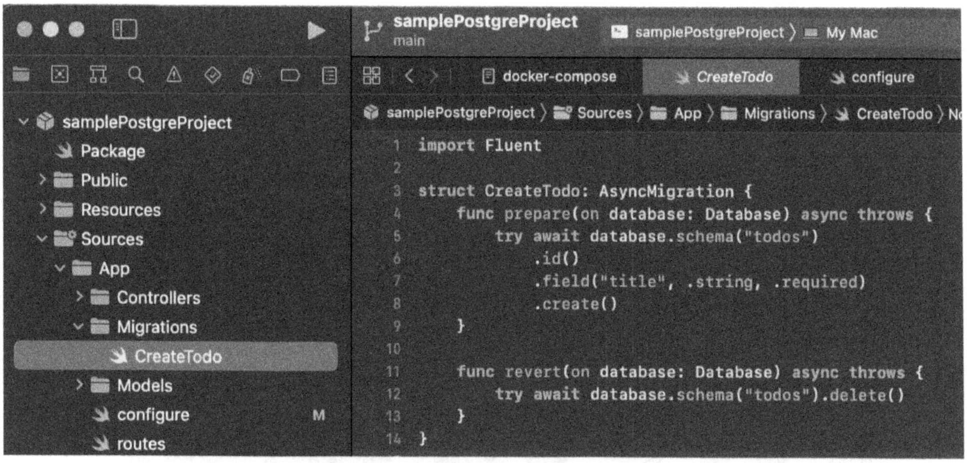

FIGURE 5.24 Migration—boilerplate.

As can be seen in this boilerplate code, this Migration is written for creating a table **todos** with **id** as the primary key and **title** as another column of type string. Furthermore, there is a **revert** function to undo the creation of this table.

As our Migration to create the **todos** table is ready, let us run this Migration. Furthermore, proceed to the terminal and type the following commands:

```
cd project directory

vapor run migrate
```

Press *Enter*, and you will see an output as shown in the following figure:

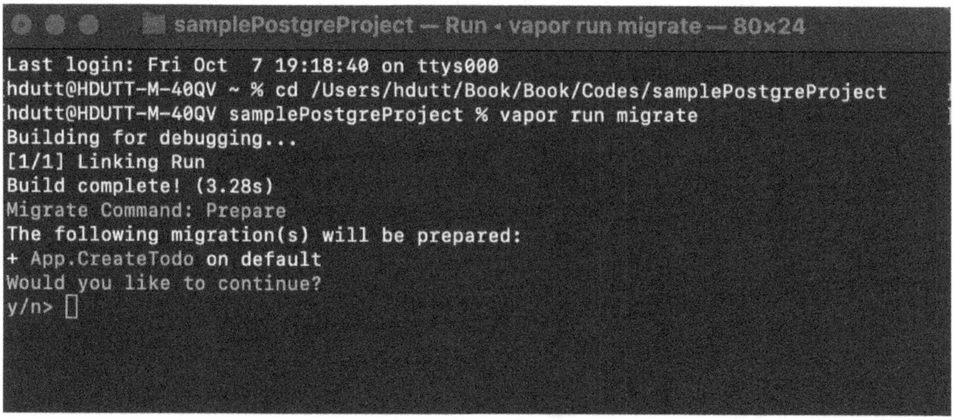

FIGURE 5.25 Run the Migration.

As is evident, it is asking permission to run Migration **CreateTodo**. Type **y** and press *Enter*. This will run the Migration and create a **todos** table in **newpostgredb**, as shown in the following figure:

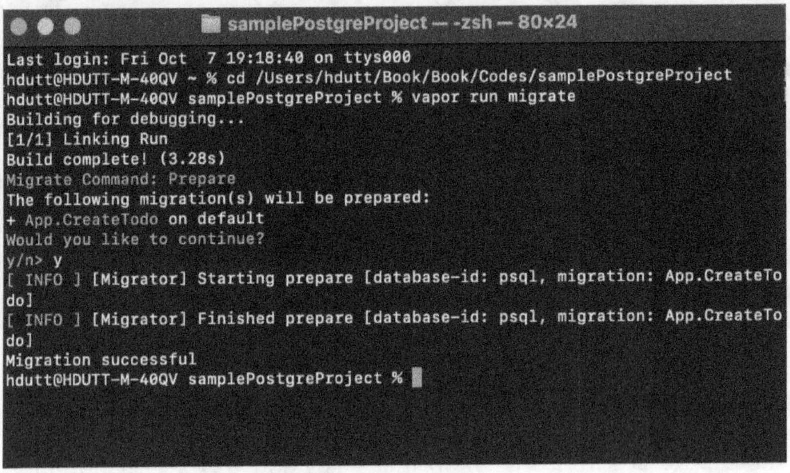

FIGURE 5.26 Migration complete.

Excellent! Our first Migration is now complete. However, how can we visually inspect the table and data?

POSTICO

Postico is an application that provides an easy-to-use visual interface for making Postgres more accessible to users, whether newcomers or specialists. To install this application, visit *https://eggerapps.at/postico/* and press the download button, as shown in the following figure:

FIGURE 5.27 Download Postico.

After the application gets downloaded, move it to the **Applications** folder and launch the app. It will launch a user interface, as shown in the following figure:

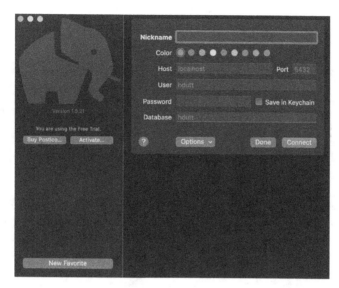

FIGURE 5.28 Launch Postico.

As we are using **localhost** and port **5432**, we need not change anything and press **Connect** button. This will open the **newpostgredb,** as shown in the following figure:

FIGURE 5.29 Open DB.

As can be seen in the following figure, it has opened **hdutt** DB, but we need to open **newpostgredb**. To do that, click on the **localhost** button with the elephant icon highlighted in red. This will take us to the page where we can select other DBs, as shown in the following figure:

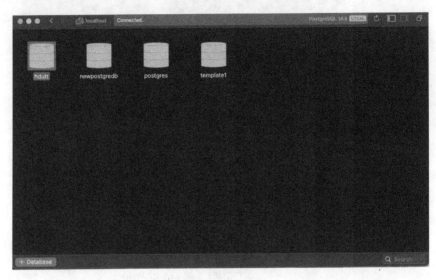

FIGURE 5.30 Select DB.

Double-click on **newpostgredb** to open the DB, as shown in the following figure:

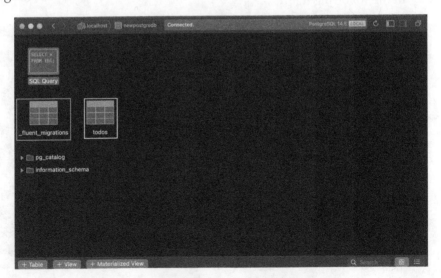

FIGURE 5.31 Open newpostgredb.

We can see two tables here: **_fluent_migrations** and **todos**. **todos** is the table we created, but what is **_fluent_migrations**?

_fluent_migrations is the table that holds the history of migrations on the table. Double-click on **_fluent_migrations** to open the table, as shown in the following figure:

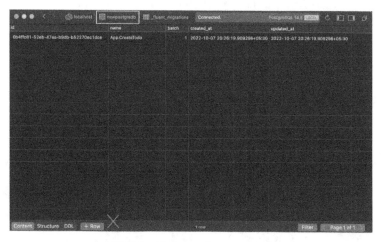

FIGURE 5.32 Open _fluent_migrations.

Never update this table directly, as one Migration only runs once, and updating this will lead to the corruption of Migration data. To go back to the table list, click on **newpostgredb,** and then double-click on the **todos** table to open the DB, as shown in the following figure:

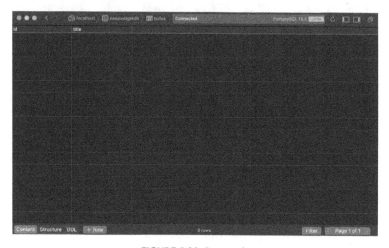

FIGURE 5.33 Open todos.

As we can now verify, the **todos** table has been created with **id** as the primary column and **title** as another column.

CREATE AND SAVE MODEL

After creating the table, we will have to save data into the table, and therefore, we need a model that can map data to the schema of the table.

Create Model

The boilerplate code also has a boilerplate code for the **todo** model, which can be found under the **Model** folder, as shown in the following figure:

FIGURE 5.34 Todo model.

As shown in *Figure 5.34*, a **Todo** model class conforms to both **Model** and **Content** protocols. We will use property wrappers in lines 7 and 10 to map table columns to the associated model properties.

NOTE   *At line 10, the title in the key value is the actual table column name. This should not be confused with the property name title of the Todo model.*

Save Model

To understand how we can save our **Todo** model in the database, let us again take advantage of the boilerplate code provided by Vapor. Open **TodoController** in the **Controller,** as shown in the following figure:

FIGURE 5.35 TodoController.

We have already gone through the concepts of **RouteCollection**, **Routes**, **Encode/ Decode**, and so on; therefore, we will not revisit those. As can be seen in this boilerplate **TodoController** class, there is an **index** route to get all **Todo** entries from the table. Then there is a create route to save a **Todo** model into the database and, lastly, a delete route to delete entries from the table.

We will register this controller in **routes.swift**, as shown in the following figure:

FIGURE 5.36 routes.swift.

Excellent! We have come a long way so far. Now let us run the code and test the APIs. Press *Cmd + R* or the **Play** button in Xcode to run the project. As soon as you see the following log in the console, your server is up and running.

```
[ NOTICE ] Server starting at http://127.0.0.1:8080
```

Open the browser, type the URL **http://localhost:8080/todos** in the address bar, and press *Enter*. You might get an error like shown in the following figure:

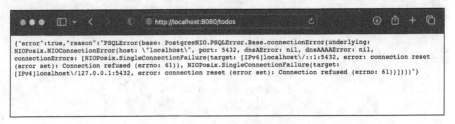

FIGURE 5.37 Browser error.

A closer look into the error shows that the Postgres server is not running. You can verify that by clicking the Postgres app icon in the status bar, as shown in the following figure:

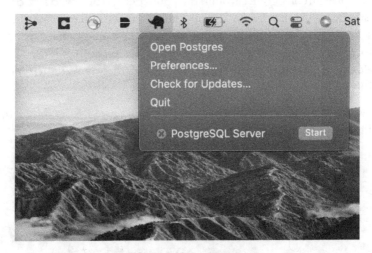

FIGURE 5.38 Postgres server.

Click the start button and start the Postgres server and hit the URL **http://localhost:8080/todos** again. This time we will get an empty response array, as shown in *Figure 5.39*, as we do not have any data in the database yet, as shown in the following:

FIGURE 5.39 Server running.

Now it is time to test the APIs. Launch **Postman.app** to post **Todo** objects and save them in the database, as shown in the following figure:

FIGURE 5.40 Post request.

Press the **Send** button to execute the **POST** request. This will result in success with status **200 OK**, as shown in the following figure:

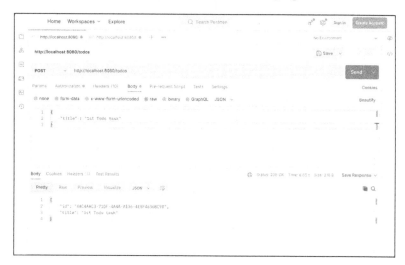

FIGURE 5.41 Create Todo response.

To test it against the **GET** request, open a new tab in Postman and create a **GET** request, as shown in the following figure:

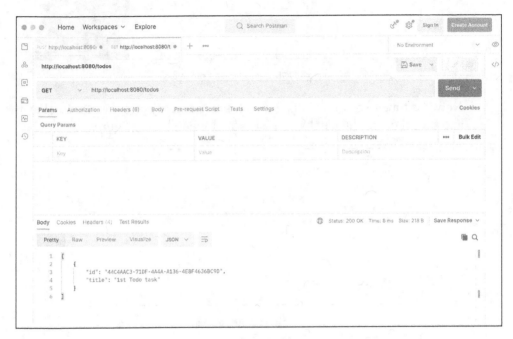

FIGURE 5.42 GET request.

As can be seen in *Figure 5.42*, we got the same title back in the response, which we saved in the **POST** request. We can also test it in the browser by again typing the URL **http://localhost:8080/todos** in the address bar and hitting *Enter*. This time we will get a response as shown in the following figure:

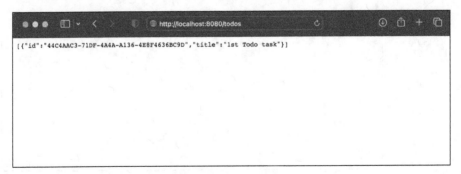

FIGURE 5.43 Browser test.

Excellent! With this, we are done with the basics of creating a **Model** and saving the data in a persistent store using Fluent ORM. From here, you can try different APIs to update, delete, and so on, on data.

CONCLUSION

This chapter is a very important milestone in this book. It is the foundation block for a server that actually stores data in the persistent store. Without the capability of storing data in a persistent store, a remote server is not very useful. In this chapter, we understood the techniques to persist data with Vapor using a Postgres (PostgreSQL) database and Fluent ORM. Understanding of these concepts will be further enhanced when we study data persistence and ORM on the iOS platform. With this, we can conclude this chapter.

In the upcoming chapter, we will dive into understanding the basic building blocks of iOS UI development.

6

BUILDING USER INTERFACES FOR iOS

INTRODUCTION

In the previous chapters, we have gone through various aspects of server-side development with server-side Swift and Vapor. In *Chapter 2: Setting Up the Environment,* we touched upon the topic of client-side development with the creation of the *Hello World* project for iOS.

As we have become familiar with Swift syntax and Xcode in the previous chapters and created the **Hello World** project in *Chapter 2: Setting Up the Environment,* we can move faster in this chapter. The aim of this chapter is to understand the basic building blocks of iOS UI development and complete the circle of full-stack development with Swift.

STRUCTURE

In this chapter, we will discuss the following topics:

- Autolayout with Storyboards
- SwiftUI
  - Working with text
  - Working with images
  - Stacks

AUTO LAYOUT WITH STORYBOARDS

Developing apps that look great in all orientations and across multiple device sizes is a daunting task. In *Chapter 2: Setting Up the Environment*, *Figure 2.24: Simulator Layout mode*, recall how, in layout mode, the `Hello World` label disappeared. That happened because we did not apply Auto Layout constraints to the label. Auto Layout is the rescuer that makes it possible to support different screen sizes and orientations of iPhone and iPad devices in your apps.

Auto Layout also makes internationalization easy. We need not create new XIBs or storyboards for every language we wish to support in the app, including `right-to-left` (`RTL`) languages such as Arabic.

To understand Auto Layout, let us revisit the `Hello World` project discussed in *Chapter 2: Setting Up the Environment* and proceed to `Main.storyboard`. Select the `Hello World` label on the storyboard, as shown in the following figure. As indicated in the figure by a red arrow, the `Add New Constraints` menu is at the bottom-right of the editor. We can use this menu to add new constraints to UI elements, like the label in the following example:

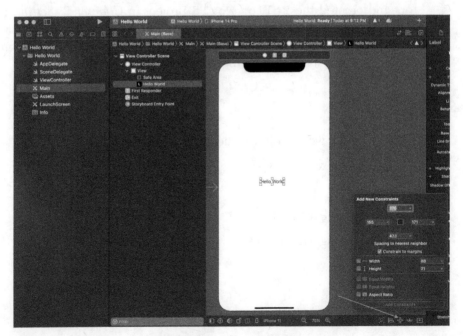

FIGURE 6.1 Add new constraint menu.

As is evident, the **Add new constraint** menu provides an option to anchor UI elements from left, right, top, and bottom. Furthermore, height and width properties can also be set along with the aspect ratio. Just left of this menu is another menu, the **Align menu**, as shown in the following figure:

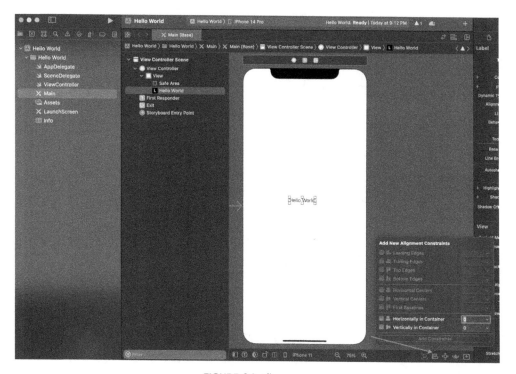

FIGURE 6.2 Align menu.

This menu is used to create alignment constraints for a UI element with respect to another UI element.

In this example, we will center align the **Hello World** label on the container view. Apart from the menus described previously, there is another way to provide alignment constraints to a UI element. Select the label on the storyboard, press the **Control Key**, and drag the mouse pointer from the label to the container view, as shown in the following figure:

FIGURE 6.3 Drag to align.

Once you release the drag on the container view, it will open a context menu, as shown in the following figure. In the context menu, you will see various alignment options. As we are interested in the central alignment of the label on the container view, we will select **Center Horizontally in Safe Area** and **Center Vertically in Safe Area**.

FIGURE 6.4 Center aligns the label.

As soon as we are done applying these constraints, the storyboard will show T-Bars around the selected UI element to visualize the applied constraints, as shown in the following figure. These T-Bars also indicate any warnings or errors in applying constraints by turning yellow or red, respectively. As shown in the following figure, there are some warnings for the constraints we have applied to the **Hello World** label:

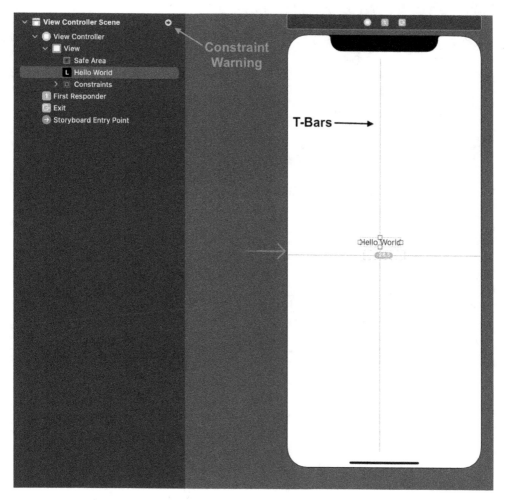

FIGURE 6.5 T-Bars.

Click on the **Constraint Warning** icon shown in the left corner of *Figure 6.5*. This will open another panel with the list of warnings and errors, as shown in the following figure:

FIGURE 6.6 Constraint warning/error panel.

In this case, the warning is about a misplaced view, which is because when we placed the label on the screen, it was not centered, but now we have applied constraints to put it in the screen's center. The actual position of the label and the constraints are conflicting here, and that is why it is showing the warning. To fix this warning, we will have to update the position of the label within the container view. Click on the warning row on the left panel in *Figure 6.6*, and this will open a pop-up panel with options to fix this warning, as shown in the following figure:

FIGURE 6.7 Fix misplacement.

In the pop-up, choose **Update frames** and press the **Fix Misplacement** button. As soon as we are done fixing the constraint warning, T-Bars will become blue, as shown in the following figure:

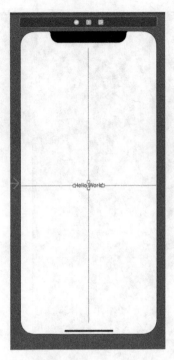

FIGURE 6.8 T-Bars without conflicts.

Run the code again and put the simulator in layout mode. This time, we will see the **Hello World** label in the center of the screen, as shown in the following figure:

FIGURE 6.9 Simulator result after fixing constraints.

So far, we have seen the process of applying constraints to a UI element with respect to whether it is a container or container view. Let us now understand the techniques involved in applying constraints between UI elements at the same hierarchy level. To start with, drag another label from the object library and place it below the **Hello World** label, as shown in the following figure:

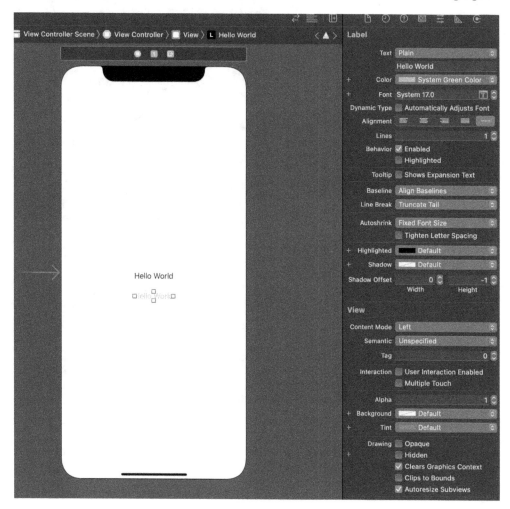

FIGURE 6.10 Add new label.

To distinguish between two **Hello World** labels, let us make a new label's text green. As we did in the previous section, press the **Control** key and drag the mouse pointer from the green label to the old **Hello World** label, as shown in the following figure:

FIGURE 6.11 Control + Drag to add constraints.

This will pop up a context menu with multiple constraint parameters to choose from, as shown in the following figure:

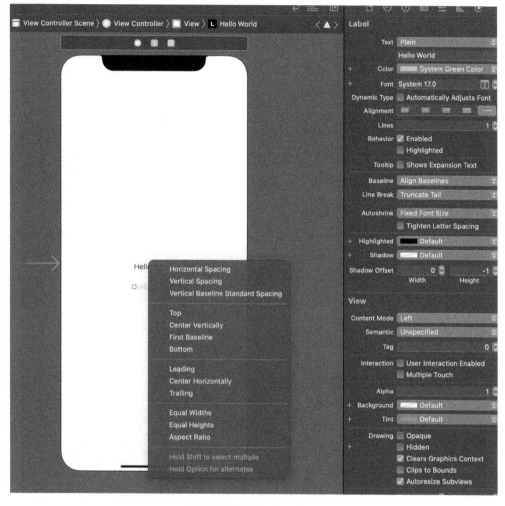

FIGURE 6.12 Align two views.

We are interested in setting vertical spacing between the two labels so that they will always be at a constant vertical distance from each other, and we want to align the leading edge of these two labels as well so that they are always aligned from the leading edge.

As we can see, **Vertical Spacing** and **Leading** constraints are available in the context menu. We will apply both of these constraints, and as soon as we do that, we can see T-Bars for the green label, as shown in the following figure:

FIGURE 6.13 T-Bars for green-colored label.

Let us run the code that will launch the simulator. We can verify the results of applying constraints in portrait mode, as shown in the following figure:

FIGURE 6.14 Constraints in portrait mode.

We can verify the results of applying constraints in layout mode, as shown in the following figure:

FIGURE 6.15 Constraints in layout mode.

We have now achieved a stable UI in both orientations. You can experiment with different UI arrangements to explore more about setting constraints on a view with respect to the container view and/or the other UI elements.

SWIFT UI

In *WWDC* 2019, Apple surprised everyone following the company's tech space by announcing a completely new framework for UI called SwiftUI. It changed the way we used to develop iOS apps. This was one of the biggest shifts in the Apple developer's ecosystem since the debut of Swift.

With SwiftUI, we can now develop the app's UI with declarative Swift syntax in Xcode. It means that we now do not need to mess around with XIBs, and writing Storyboards and UI code is similar to writing any other code in Swift.

Another landmark is the canvas and preview feature, which has always been a weak point of Xcode. With SwiftUI, we can now preview the complete UI without running the app in the simulators. And hence, with SwiftUI, we get immediate feedback on the UI we are coding. This instant preview feature simply makes UI development an easy and fun game, and we can make iterations much faster.

The new canvas also lets us design the user interface visually using drag and drop, and Xcode automatically generates the SwiftUI code as we add the UI components. This keeps the code and the UI in sync.

Starting from Xcode 11, we can choose between SwiftUI and Storyboard to build the user interface for our app, as shown in the following figure. If we have already built an app before, we can continue using Interface Builder to layout the UI on the storyboard:

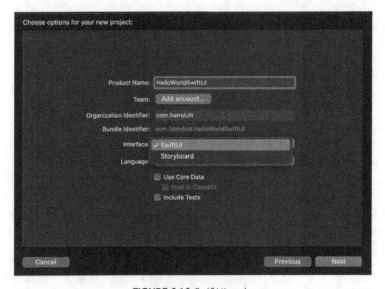

FIGURE 6.16 SwiftUI project.

With SwiftUI, Interface Builder and Storyboards are not needed. It is replaced by a code editor and a preview canvas like the one shown in the following figure. You write the code in the code editor. Xcode then renders the user interface in real-time and displays it in the canvas:

FIGURE 6.17 SwiftUI Canvas.

Working with Text

The sample code generated in **ContentView** shows you how to display a single line of text and a globe image embedded in a VStack. We will discuss all these components in detail to better understand the workings of SwiftUI.

To display text on screen, we just need to initialize a Text object and pass to it the display text, for example, **Hello World**, as already shown in *Figure 6.17.*

In SwiftUI, we can change the properties, for example, color, font, and so on, of the control by calling **Modifier** methods. For example, if we want to make the **Hello World** text bold, we can use the modifier **fontWeight** and specify bold like the following:

```
Text("Hello World").fontWeight(.bold)
```

We can chain multiple modifiers together, like, if we want to make the font rounded and specify some other parameters such as font type and size, and so on, we can specify the following:

```
Text("Hello World")

    .fontWeight(.bold)

    .font(.system(size: 20))

    .foregroundColor(Color.green)
```

Refreshing the canvas will show the updated text label, as shown in the following figure:

FIGURE 6.18 SwiftUI text properties.

While we can customize the properties of a control directly by writing code, we can also use the design canvas to edit the properties. By default, the preview runs in **Live mode**, as shown in the following figure:

FIGURE 6.19 SwiftUI Canvas modes.

To edit the view's properties, we first have to switch to **Selectable** mode. After that, hold the **Command** key and click the text to bring up the pop-over menu, as shown in the following figure:

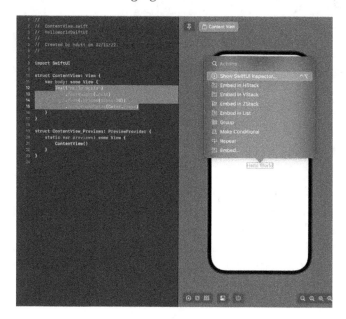

FIGURE 6.20 Inspect and edit properties 1.

Choose the **Show SwiftUI Inspector** menu, and it pops out the view for editing the text and font properties, as shown in the following figure:

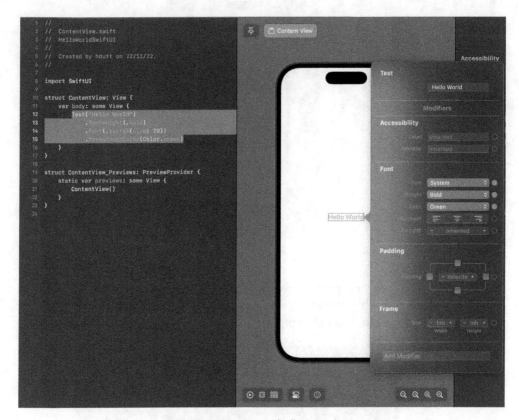

FIGURE 6.21 Inspect and edit properties 2.

The great part is that the code will update automatically upon making changes to the font properties in the edit view.

Working with Images

Other than text, images are another basic element that is being used in iOS app development. SwiftUI provides an Image class for rendering and drawing images on the screen. First, let us pull an image from the disk into the assets of the Xcode project by dragging and dropping it into the assets folder, as shown in the following figure:

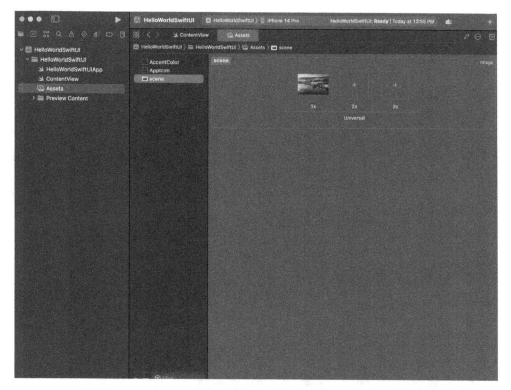

FIGURE 6.22 Sample Image.

Next are some examples to show how we work with images in SwiftUI:

```
var body: some View {

    Image("scene")

}
```

As shown in *Figure 6.23*, the image is rendered successfully on the canvas. However, the image is extending beyond the screen size, and only a portion of it is visible.

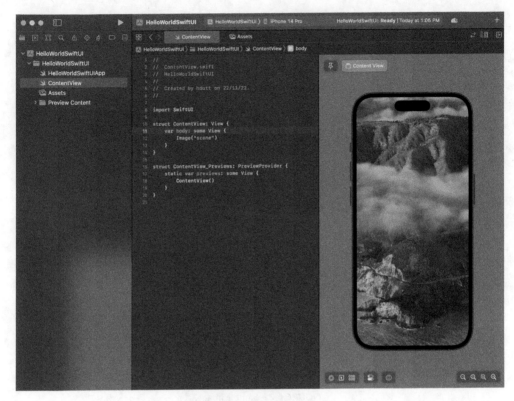

FIGURE 6.23 Render Image.

In order to fix this image size overflowing issue, we need to apply the `.resizable()` modifier as follows:

```
Image("scene") .resizable()
```

This will make it fit on the entire available screen, but as shown in the following figure, this disturbs the aspect ratio of the image:

FIGURE 6.24 Render Image within screen bounds.

To scale the image to fit within the screen and maintain its aspect ratio, we can either use the **scaledToFit** modifier as follows:

```
Image("scene")

    .resizable()

    .scaledToFit()
```

Or we can also use the **aspectRatio** modifier with **.fit** mode as follows:

```
Image("scene")

    .resizable()

    .aspectRatio(contentMode: .fit)
```

As shown in the following figure, the image looks great within the screen bounds:

FIGURE 6.25 Render Image with the preserved aspect ratio.

Let us jump on to another important element of Swift UI, that is, Stacks.

Working with Stacks

Stacks in SwiftUI are similar to the stack views in UIKit. By using different combinations of views in horizontal and vertical stacks, we can construct complex user interfaces for the apps. While working with UIKit, it is mandatory to use auto layout in order to build interfaces that fit all screen sizes, which might feel like a complicated subject and hard to learn for beginners. However, with SwiftUI, using stacks including VStack, Hstack, and Zstack, we can create complex **Uis** without learning the complexities of Auto Layout.

To understand this, let us revisit our **Text** and **Image** examples discussed in previous sections and combine them in a single UI. Let us first put the **Text** and **Image** in vertical alignment with respect to each other as follows:

```
Vstack {

    Text("Hello World")

            .fontWeight(.bold)

            .font(.system(size: 20))

            .foregroundColor(Color.green)

    Image("scene")

            .resizable()

            .scaledToFit()

    Spacer()

}
```

As shown in the following figure, the **Text** label and **Image** are aligned vertically on the screen:

FIGURE 6.26 Vstack.

Similarly, if we want to place these two UI elements horizontally with respect to each other, we can use **Hstack** as follows:

```
Hstack {

    Text("Hello World")

        .fontWeight(.bold)

        .font(.system(size: 20))

        .foregroundColor(Color.green)

    Image("scene")

        .resizable()

        .scaledToFit()

    Spacer()

}
```

As shown in the following figure, the **Text** label and **Image** are aligned horizontally on the screen:

FIGURE 6.27 Hstack.

This is working out great. What if we want to place **Text** on top of the **Image**. In this case, we can use **Zstack** to overlay **Text** over the **Image** component as follows:

```
Zstack {

    Image("scene")

        .resizable()

        .scaledToFit()

    Text("Hello World")

        .fontWeight(.bold)

        .font(.system(size: 20))

        .foregroundColor(Color.green)

    Spacer()

}
```

As shown in the following figure, **Text** is overlayed over **Image** on the screen:

FIGURE 6.28 Zstack.

We have understood the basics of **Storyboard** with **Autolayout** as well as **SwiftUI**. We are good with the basics of UI development on iOS. Next, let us look at the basics of data storage and management on iOS using the CoreData framework.

CONCLUSION

In this chapter, we learned about the basic building blocks of iOS UI development and are now inching closer to completing the circle of full-stack development with Swift. We have touched on the basics of two available frameworks for iOS UI development, namely, UIKit and SwiftUI. It is expected that the readers will go deep into the functioning of these frameworks to be able to appreciate these powerful UI development frameworks fully.

Next, we will understand two more important building blocks of iOS app development, that is, CoreData and networking frameworks, in the upcoming chapter before proceeding to the development of our first app.

DATA PERSISTENCE WITH CORE DATA AND SQLITE IN IOS

INTRODUCTION

In the previous chapter, we learned about the various UI aspects of the iOS app. Apart from the UI, an iOS app also deals with data for offline use and data persistence.

STRUCTURE

In this chapter, we will discuss the following topics:

- Core Data
  - Core Data stack
  - Include Core Data in a new project
  - Include Core Data in an existing project
  - CRUD operations
  - Core Data migrations
- Lightweight data migration
- Networking

CORE DATA

Core Data is an object graph and persistence framework developed by Apple for the macOS and iOS platforms. It provides the capability to serialize data organized by the relational entity-attribute model into XML, binary, or SQLite files.

We can use Core Data to save the application's permanent data for offline use, cache temporary data, and/or add undo functionality for the app on the device. In case sync of data across multiple devices is needed for a single iCloud account, Core Data automatically mirrors the schema to the CloudKit container.

Through Core Data's Data model editor, we define the data types and relationships and generate respective class definitions.

Core Data Stack

Core Data provides a set of classes that collaboratively create a Core Data stack, given as follows:

- **NSManagedObjectModel** describes the app's types, including their properties and relationships. A Core Data application has a data model that describes the data of the application. An instance of the **NSManagedObjectModel** class loads the data model and exposes it to the Core Data stack. When the Core Data stack of the application is set up, the managed object model loads the data model from the application bundle. It is comparable to the schema of a database.

- **NSManagedObjectContext** tracks changes to instances of your app's types. An instance of the **NSManagedObjectContext** class is the slate of the Core Data stack. It keeps a reference to the persistent store coordinator, and a developer very rarely interacts with the managed object model or the persistent store coordinator.

- **NSPersistentStoreCoordinator** saves and fetches instances of your app's types from stores. The persistent store coordinator is like the glue of the Core Data stack. It keeps a reference to the managed object model and the managed object context, and it is in charge of the persistent storage of the application.

We can use the **NSPersistentContainer** instance to set up the model, context, and store coordinator simultaneously.

Include Core Data in a New Project

We can include Core Data in the project at the time of creating it by clicking the **Use Core Data** checkbox, as shown in the following figure:

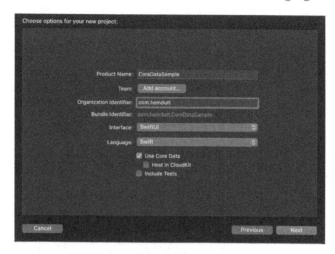

FIGURE 7.1 Include Core Data in a new project.

Once the project is created, we will see a file named **CoreDataSample. xcdatamodeld** added to the project.

On clicking it, we will see tools to configure entities that represent data models, as shown in the following figure:

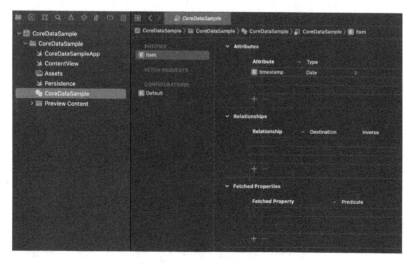

FIGURE 7.2 CoreDataSample.xcdatamodeld.

Include Core Data in an Existing Project

While it is easier to add a Core Data framework at the time of creating the project, it is possible to add a Core Data framework to the project at some later stage. Steps to add Core Data to an existing project are listed as follows:

1. Open the project in Xcode and right-click on the project folder. Click **New File** in the context menu, as shown in the following figure:

FIGURE 7.3 New file.

2. This will pop up the file template selection window. Choose the **Data Model** from the templates, as shown in the following figure:

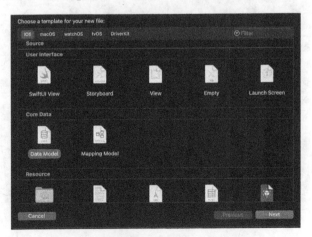

FIGURE 7.4 Data model.

3. Click on the **Next** button and name the data model as shown in the following figure:

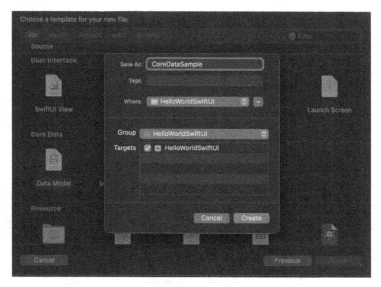

FIGURE 7.5 CoreDataSample.

4. Click the **Create** button, and, finally, the new **CoreDataSample. xcdatamodel** file will be created as shown in the following figure:

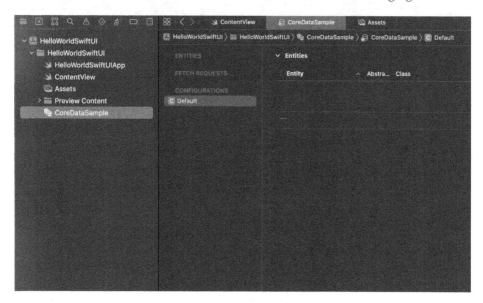

FIGURE 7.6 CoreDataSample.xcdatamodeld.

CRUD Operations

For understanding CRUD operations with the **CoreData** framework, let us study the sample project **CoreDataSample** created in the section titled *Include Core Data in a new project*. There are two things to be noted in this Xcode project template:

1. A new file named **CoreDataSample.xcdatamodeld**

2. The **Persistence.swift** file with Core Data Stack code

First, let us check **CoreDataSample.xcdatamodeld**. Here you will notice an entity named **Item** with only one attribute, that is, a **timestamp**, which is of type **Date**, as shown in the following figure:

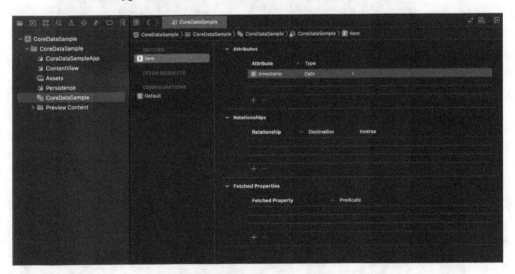

FIGURE 7.7 Core Data entity.

You can add more attributes using the **+** button in the **Attributes** section. There are other sections on the window as well that define the relationships between entities and their fetch properties.

Relationships in Core Data: In Core Data, relationships define how entities are connected to each other. There are three types of relationships: to-one, to-many, and many-to-many. Here is an example to illustrate these relationship types:

Consider Two Entities: "Department" and "Employee." Each department can have multiple employees, while each employee belongs to a single department. This represents a too-many relationships from the "Department" entity to the "Employee" entity and a to-one relationship from the "Employee" entity to the "Department" entity.

Fetching Properties using Relationships: Fetching properties in Core Data involves retrieving specific data based on certain criteria or conditions. Let us explore how properties can be fetched using relationships with the above example.

1. **Fetching All Employees in a Department**: Suppose we want to fetch all employees working in a particular department. We can use the relationship property defined in the "Department" entity to retrieve the associated employees. Here is an example code snippet:

```
let departmentFetchRequest: NSFetchRequest<Department> =
Department.fetchRequest()

departmentFetchRequest.predicate = NSPredicate(format:
"name == %@", "Sales")


do {

  let departments = try context.fetch(departmentFetchRequest)

  if let salesDepartment = departments.first {

    if let employees = salesDepartment.employees {

      for employee in employees {

        // Access employee properties

        print(employee.name)

        // Perform operations with employee data

      }

    }

  }

} catch {

    print("Error fetching departments: \(error.
    localizedDescription)")

}
```

2. **Fetching Department of an Employee:** To fetch the department associated with a specific employee, we can use the inverse relationship property defined in the "Employee" entity. Here is an example code snippet:

```
let employeeFetchRequest: NSFetchRequest<Employee> = Employee.
fetchRequest()

employeeFetchRequest.predicate = NSPredicate(format: "name ==
%@", "John Doe")


do {

    let employees = try context.fetch(employeeFetchRequest)

    if let johnDoe = employees.first {

      if let department = johnDoe.department {

        // Access department properties

        print(department.name)

        // Perform operations with department data

      }

    }

} catch {

  print("Error fetching employees: \(error.
  localizedDescription)")

}
```

In both examples, we utilize the relationships defined in the data model to access the associated objects and their properties. These relationships enable us to efficiently fetch and manipulate related data in Core Data.

In essence, Core Data relationships allow developers to establish connections between entities, providing a powerful mechanism for modeling complex data relationships. By leveraging these relationships, developers can fetch properties and navigate through the associated data, enhancing the flexibility and efficiency of data retrieval in Core Data.

As shown in the following figure, in the right panel of Xcode, you can see more details about the entity. The most important attribute in this window is the **Codegen** section, which shows a dropdown with the default value of **Class Definition**.

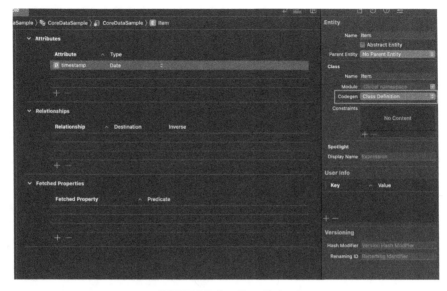

FIGURE 7.8 Core Data Codegen.

If you click on the **Codegen** dropdown, you will see two more options, as shown in the following figure:

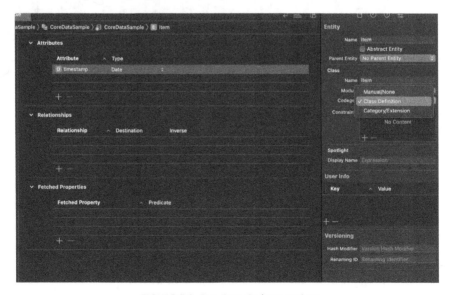

FIGURE 7.9 Core Data Codegen options.

Codegen

The Codegen setting implemented by Apple in the Xcode data model editor is to help developers manage and maintain their **NSManagedObject** subclasses. The Codegen setting has three possible configurations:

Manual/None

This was the default behavior prior to Xcode 8: to manually create and maintain the changes to the **NSManagedObject** subclasses. We have to click on **Create NSManagedObject Subclass** manually, as shown in the following figure:

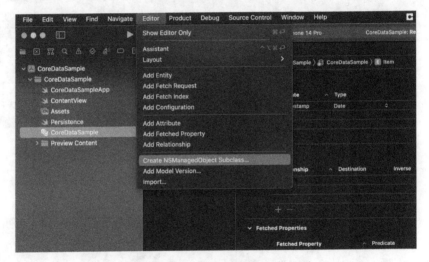

FIGURE 7.10 Core Data Codegen manual.

If you follow the step correctly, Xcode will generate two files for a newly created entity (for example, **Item** entity):

```
Item+CoreDataClass.swift
```

```
Item+CoreDataProperties.swift
```

Class Definition

This configuration is the default **Codegen** configuration when you create an entity in the data model editor. With this configuration, Xcode will automatically generate the required **NSManagedObject** subclass for the project. To see the auto-generated file, *cmd* + click on the entity (in our case, **Item**), then select **Jump to Definition** as shown in the following figure:

FIGURE 7.11 Autogenerated Core Data Class 1.

Right-click on the opened **Item+CoreDataClass.swift** and select **Navigate |Show in Finder,** as shown in the following figure:

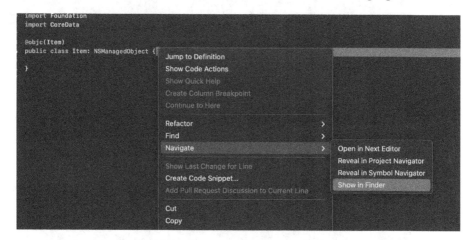

FIGURE 7.12 Autogenerated Core Data Class 2.

You will find both **Item+CoreDataClass.swift** and **Item+CoreData Properties.swift** in the finder.

NOTE   *Autogenerated files are not located in the Xcode project but in the Derived Data folder of Xcode. That is why you should never edit the auto-generated files, as they are managed by Xcode, and therefore, they will be overwritten by Xcode every time you build the project.*

Category/Extension

This configuration is a trade-off between Class Definition and Manual/None. Xcode will automatically generate only **Item+CoreDataProperties. swift**, and you will have to manage and maintain **Item+CoreDataClass. swift** yourself.

Moving to **Persistence.swift**, we can observe the template code for the Core Data Stack. As shown in the following figure, **Persistence.swift** has an **init** function in which we are creating the Core Data Stack:

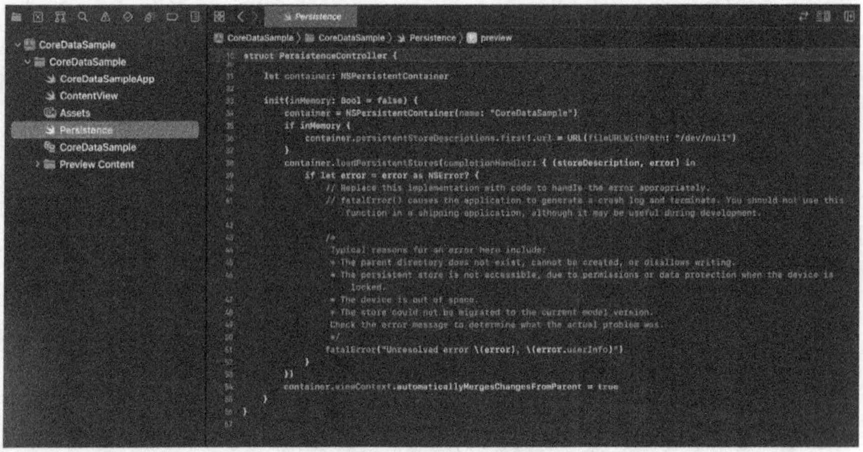

FIGURE 7.13 Core Data stack.

Next, let us look at **ContentView.swift**. At this point, in the template code, you will see the setting up of **NSManagedObjectContext** for the **ContentView** and Crud operations, as shown in the following figure:

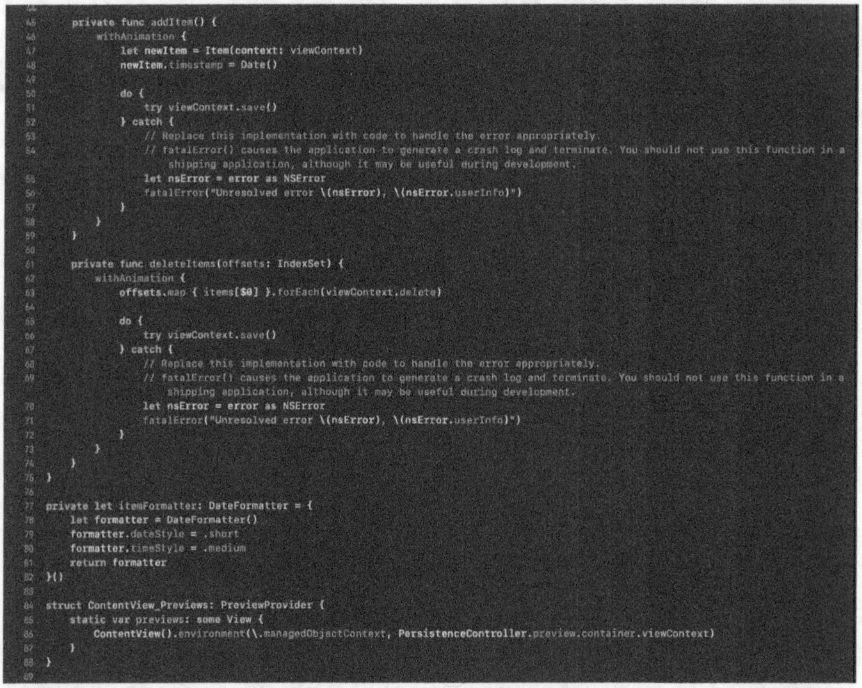

FIGURE 7.14 CRUD operations.

Checking the template code in the preview will show up the UI with data fetched from the database, as shown in the following figure:

FIGURE 7.15 DB operation and UI.

Core Data Migrations

In the development phase of a project, we keep adding new features with every new version of the app. These features might include new business requirements that need to update our data models and entities.

In order to do core data migration, we need to keep on versioning our **.xcdatamodeld** file rather than making new changes to the existing data model. There are two types of migrations available.

■ Automatic data migration or lightweight migration. Lightweight migration refers to the migration automatically done based on the differences between the source and destination managed object models.

■ Heavyweight migration is the manual migration that handles cases when changes to the data model go beyond the capabilities of lightweight migration, such as the split of data from one column into more than one column.

LIGHTWEIGHT DATA MIGRATION

Automatic or lightweight migration can be used in the following cases:

- Add an entity
- Remove an entity
- Renaming an entity
- Add an attribute
- Remove an attribute
- Renaming an attribute
- Add a relationship
- Remove a relationship
- Renaming a relationship

To execute a lightweight migration, we need to go through the following steps:

1. Navigate to the **Editor** |**Add Model Version,** as shown in the following figure:

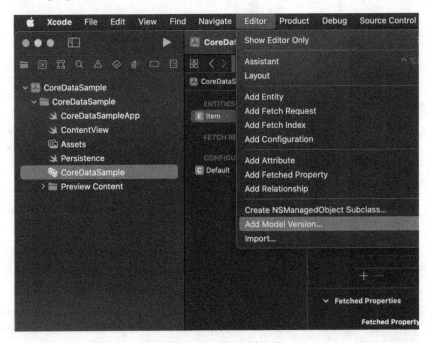

FIGURE 7.16 Add model version.

2. Step 1 will prompt a modal window where you can name your new model and select on which model you want to base your new model version, as shown in the following figure:

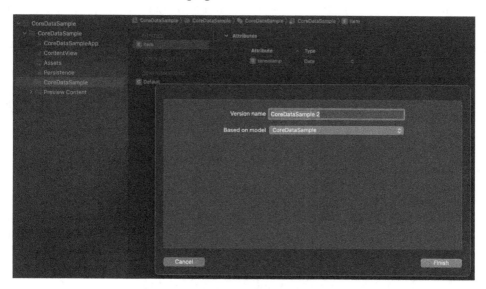

FIGURE 7.17 Version model.

3. This will create another model, **CoreDataSample 2.xcdatamodel,** based on **CoreDataSample.xcdatamodel**, as shown in the following figure. Furthermore, notice in the rightmost panel, under **Model Version**, that the current version is still **CoreDataSample**, which we need to change to **CoreDataSample 2** to make the new version operational with the new code:

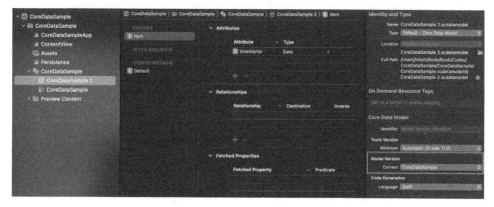

FIGURE 7.18 New version model.

That is all for the lightweight migration, and most of the model changes in the project can be catered to through lightweight migration. However, there are certain cases where migration needs to be manually defined, and therefore, data model migration also needs to be manually done. For example, let us consider a scenario of a name attribute in an entity where the attribute is now split into two attributes, namely, first name and last name. This situation cannot be handled by automatic migration, and we need to implement a data model and migration model manually.

To study heavyweight migration in detail, please visit *https://developer.apple.com/documentation/coredata/heavyweight_migration*

NETWORKING

More often than not, an iOS app is not a standalone app and needs to communicate with a remote server for various of its functional features. Whether it retrieves application data from a server, updates a status, or downloads remote files to disk, network requests are an essential aspect of an iOS app. To help with the many requirements and use cases for network requests, Apple provides **URLSession**, a complete networking API.

Before we begin, it is important to understand **URLSession** and its constituent classes. **URLSession** is the key object responsible for sending and receiving requests to and from a remote server. We create it with **URLSessionConfiguration**, which can be further categorized as follows:

- **default:** Creates a **configuration** object that uses disk-persisted global cache, credential, and cookie storage objects.

- **ephemeral:** Similar to the default configuration, but stores all of the session-related data in memory. This is like a *private* session.

- **background:** This configuration lets the session perform upload or download tasks in the background. Data transfers continue even when the app itself is suspended or terminated by the system.

Another important class **URLSessionTask** is an abstract class that denotes a task object. A session creates one or more tasks to do the actual work of fetching data and uploading or downloading files.

There are the following three types of session tasks:

1. **URLSessionDataTask**: This task is used for **GET** requests to retrieve data from remote servers.

2. **URLSessionUploadTask**: This task is used to upload a file from disk to a remote server using a service via a **POST** or **PUT** method.

3. **URLSessionDownloadTask**: This task is used to download a file from a remote service to a temporary file location.

We can also suspend, resume, and cancel tasks. **URLSessionDownloadTask** also has the extra ability to pause for future resumption.

URLSession can return data in two ways: either via a completion handler when a task finishes, either successfully or with an error, or by calling methods on a delegate that we can set when we create the session.

PROTOCOL SUPPORT

The **URLSession** class off the shelf supports the data, file, FTP, HTTP, and HTTPS URL schemes, with transparent support for proxy servers and SOCKS gateways, as configured in the user's system preferences.

We can also add support for proprietary networking protocols and URL schemes by subclassing **URLProtocol**.

iOS 9.0 and macOS 10.11 onwards require **App Transport Security** (**ATS**) for all HTTP connections made with **URLSession**, which requires that HTTP connections use HTTPS.

Enough of the theory. We will see **URLSession** in action in the upcoming chapter, where we will create our full-stack project.

CONCLUSION

In this chapter, we learned about data persistence using the Core Data framework for iOS applications. In the process, we learned about CRUD operations and data migrations with the Core Data framework. We also touched on the basics of networking using **URLSession** for iOS applications to perform communication with a remote server. Next will be the most important chapter of this book, where we will implement our full-stack project.

8

FULL-STACK IMPLEMENTATION

INTRODUCTION

Thus far, we have learned all the basic principles and architectures involved in Vapor and iOS apps. However, all these topics were discussed in isolation to make it simple for you to grab specific concepts easily. In this chapter, we will implement a full-stack iOS app to execute the knowledge gained so far.

STRUCTURE

In this chapter, we will discuss the following topics:

- Project outline
- Setup remote database
- Server app
  - Models
  - Migrations
  - Controllers
  - Config and routes
- iOS App
  - Models
  - Networking
  - User interface
- Test run

OBJECTIVES

Thus far, we have learned all the basic principles and architectures involved in Vapor and iOS apps. We implemented small sample codes to understand working on the Vapor and iOS apps. All these samples were discussed in isolation to make it simple for you to grab specific concepts without worrying about the larger picture. In this chapter, we will specifically look into the larger picture and the full-stack implementation of an app.

PROJECT OUTLINE

For the purpose of implementing a full-stack project, let us first discuss an outline for the proposed project. In this chapter, we will create a sample project where users can add **Restaurants** and their reviews through the iOS app. Furthermore, if there is restaurant data available on the server, it should be synced with the iOS app, and more reviews can be added to those **Restaurants**.

SETUP REMOTE DATABASE

We will not go into the nitty-gritty of this process, as this has already been discussed in *Chapter 5: Persist Data, ORM and Models—Vapor.*

1. Open **Postgres.app** and create a server.

2. Create a database named **restaurantdb**, as shown in the following figure:

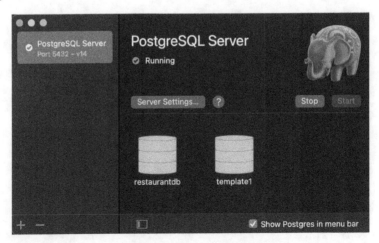

FIGURE 8.1 restaurantdb database.

3. Open **Postico.app** and create new tables named **restaurant** and **review**s in **restaurantdb**, as shown in the following figure:

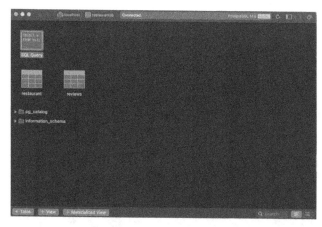

FIGURE 8.2 New tables in restaurantdb.

4. For the **restaurant** table, we will create four columns:

i. **id**: Autogenerated, primary key, integer

ii. **title**: String

iii. **poster**: String (this will store the image as a base64 string)

iv. **address**: String

For the purpose of testing, let us create one row in this table, as shown in the following figure:

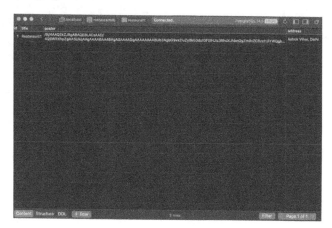

FIGURE 8.3 The restaurant table.

5. Similarly, for the **reviews** table, we will create four columns:

   i. **id**: Autogenerated, primary key, int

   ii. **title**: String

   iii. **body**: String (this will store the image as a base64 string)

   iv. **restaurant_id**: A foreign key pointing to the id column of the restaurant table

   For the purpose of testing, let us create two reviews in this table, as shown in the following figure:

FIGURE 8.4 The reviews table.

Excellent! As our database is setup, let us move on to another task, which is to create a server app that can interact with this database to perform CRUD operations in these tables.

SERVER APP

Furthermore, the basics of creating a vapor project are already covered in *Chapter 2: Setting Up the Environment*; therefore, we will not revisit them again here. Open the terminal, and

1. Create a new Vapor project named "**Restaurant-Server**".

2. Include Fluent.

3. Include Postgres DB.

4. Include Leaf.

The commands in the terminal for Steps 1–4 will look as shown in the following figure:

```
● ● ●                    🎬 Codes — -zsh — 80×24
Last login: Mon Dec 26 16:04:25 on ttys000
[hdutt@HDUTT-M-40QV ~ % cd /Users/hdutt/Desktop/movies-app-server-and-swiftui-app]
/movies-app-server
[hdutt@HDUTT-M-40QV movies-app-server % open package.swift              ]
[hdutt@HDUTT-M-40QV movies-app-server % cd /Users/hdutt/Book/Book/Codes ]
[hdutt@HDUTT-M-40QV Codes % vapor new Restaurant-Server                 ]
Cloning template...
name: Restaurant-Server
Would you like to use Fluent? (--fluent/--no-fluent)
y/n> y
fluent: Yes
db: Postgres (Recommended)
Would you like to use Leaf? (--leaf/--no-leaf)
y/n> y
leaf: Yes
Generating project files
+ Package.swift
+ main.swift
+ configure.swift
+ routes.swift
+ Todo.swift
+ CreateTodo.swift
+ .gitkeep
+ TodoController.swift
```

FIGURE 8.5 Create Restaurant-Server.

To open the project in Xcode, in the terminal, type the following:

```
Open package.swift
```

This will open the **Restaurant-Server** project in Xcode, as shown in the following figure:

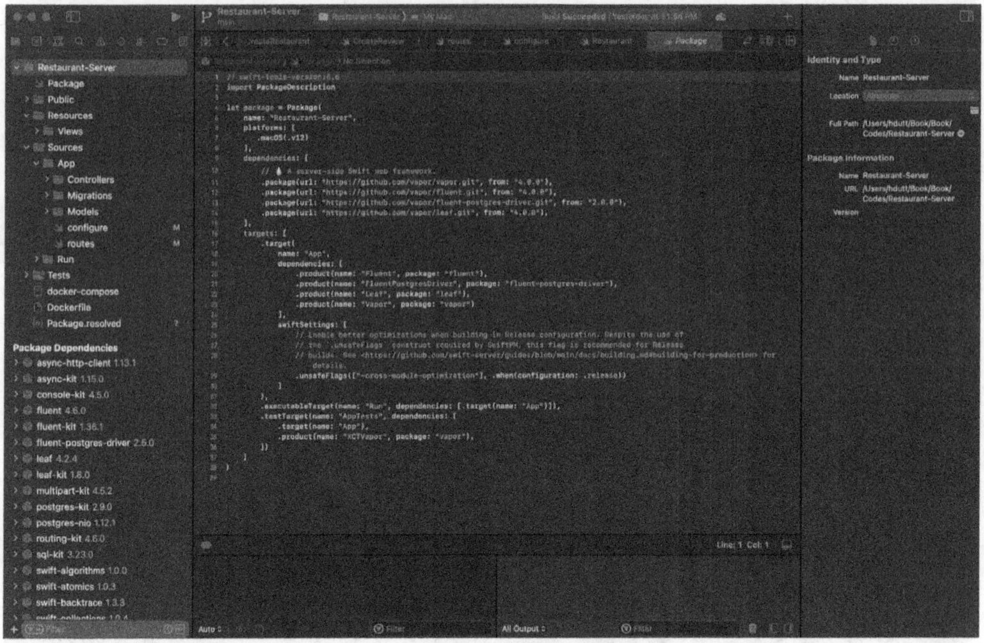

FIGURE 8.6 Restaurant-Server.

Models

Let us create models for **Restaurant** and **Reviews**, which will map to the database schema as follows:

1. Create a new group called **Models**.

2. Under this group, add a new file **Restaurant.swift**.

3. Inside the file, import **Fluent** and **Vapor**:

   ```
   import Fluent

   import Vapor
   ```

4. Create a final class **Restaurant**:

   ```
   final class Restaurant: Model, Content {

   }
   ```

5. Inside the class, create fields to map the schema in the restaurant database. The class will finally look like the following:

```
import Fluent

import Vapor

final class Restaurant: Model, Content {

    static let schema = "restaurant"


    @ID(custom: "id", generatedBy: .database) var id: Int?


    @Field(key: "title")

    var title: String


    @Field(key: "poster")

    var poster: String


    @Field(key: "address")

    var address: String


    @Children(for: \.$restaurant)

    var reviews: [Review]

    init() { }

    init(id: Int? = nil, title: String, address: String, poster:
    String) {

        self.id = id

        self.title = title

        self.address = address

        self.poster = poster

    }

}
```

6. Similarly, create another file, **Review.swift** and a model class for review inside the **Model** group.

7. Inside the **Review.swift** file, create the review model as follows:

```
import Foundation

import Vapor

import Fluent

import FluentPostgresDriver


final class Review: Model, Content {

  static let schema = "reviews"

  @ID(custom: "id", generatedBy: .database)

  var id: Int?


  @Field(key: "title")

  var title: String


  @Field(key: "body")

  var body: String


  @Parent(key: "restaurant_id")

  var restaurant: Restaurant init() { }

  init(id: Int? = nil, title: String, body: String,

  restaurantId: Int) {

    self.id = id

    self.title = title
```

```
    self.body = body

    self.$restaurant.id = restaurantId

  }



  }
```

Migrations

Next, let us write migrations for the models we created in the previous section, which will come in handy when you extend this project.

1. Create another group, **Migrations**.

2. Inside the group, create migration for the **Restaurant** model by creating a new file **CreateRestaurant.swift**.

3. Inside **CreateRestaurant.swift**, write migration for the **Restaurant** as follows:

```swift
import Foundation

import Fluent

import FluentPostgresDriver


struct CreateRestaurant: Migration {


  func prepare(on database: Database) -> EventLoopFuture<Void> {
    database.schema("restaurant") // table name

    .id()

    .field("title", .string)

    .field("poster", .string)

    .field("address", .string)

    .create()

  }
```

```
// undo

func revert(on database: Database) -> EventLoopFuture<Void> {
database.schema("Restaurant").delete() // drop the table

}


}
```

4. Similarly, create another file, **CreateReview.swift**, to write migration for **Review**:

```
import Foundation

import Vapor

import Fluent

import FluentPostgresDriver


struct CreateReview: Migration {

  func prepare(on database: Database) -> EventLoopFuture<Void> {
    database.schema("reviews")

      .id()

      .field("subject", .string)

      .field("body", .string)

      .field("restaurant_id", .int64, .references
      ("restaurant", "id"))

      .create()

}


  func revert(on database: Database) -> EventLoopFuture<Void> {
  database.schema("reviews").delete()

  }


}
```

5. The project structure should look as shown in the following figure:

FIGURE 8.7 Create models and migration.

Controllers

After the model and migrations, let us jump on the controllers where the logic will reside:

1. Create a group called **Controllers**.

2. Create a new file, **RestaurantController.swift**, in the group.

3. Inside **RestaurantController.swift**, write the controller logic as follows:

```
import Fluent

import Vapor


final class RestaurantController {
```

```swift
func create(_ req: Request) throws -> EventLoopFuture
<Restaurant> {

    let restaurant = try req.content.decode(Restaurant.self)
    return restaurant.create(on: req.db).map { restaurant }

}


func all(_ req: Request) throws ->
EventLoopFuture<[Restaurant]> {

    Restaurant.query(on: req.db).all()

}


// /restaurant/:restaurantId/reviews

func getById(_ req: Request) throws ->
EventLoopFuture<Restaurant> {


    Restaurant.query(on: req.db).filter(.id, .equal,
    req.parameters.get("restaurantId", as: UUID.self)
    ).with(\.$reviews).first().unwrap(or: Abort(.notFound))



}


func delete(_ req: Request) throws ->
EventLoopFuture<HTTPStatus> {


    Restaurant.find(req.parameters.get("restaurantId"), on:
    req.db).unwrap(or: Abort(.notFound))
        .flatMap {
            $0.delete(on: req.db)
        }.transform(to: .ok)

}

}
```

4. Similarly, create another file, **ReviewsController.swift**, to write controller logic for **Review** as follows:

```
import Foundation

import Vapor

import Fluent


final class ReviewsController {


  func create(_ req: Request) throws -> EventLoopFuture<Review>

  {


    let review = try req.content.decode(Review.self)

    return review.save(on: req.db).map { review }


  }


  func getByRestaurantId(_ req: Request) throws ->
  EventLoopFuture<[Review]> {


    guard let restaurantId = req.parameters.
    get("restaurantId", as: Int.self) else {

      throw Abort(.notFound)

    }


    return Review.query(on: req.db).filter(\.$restaurant.$id,

    .equal, restaurantId)
```

```
        .with(\.$restaurant)

        .all()



    }



    }
```

5. After this, the project structure will look as shown in the following figure:

FIGURE 8.8 Create controllers.

Config and Routes

At last, we are at the stage of updating the configuration as per our project needs and creating routes for the server:

1. Proceed to the **configure.swift** file and update the configuration as follows:

```
import Fluent
```

```swift
import FluentPostgresDriver

import Leaf

import Vapor


// configures your application
public func configure(_ app: Application) throws {
  // uncomment to serve files from /Public folder
  // app.middleware.use(FileMiddleware(publicDirectory: app.
  directory.publicDirectory))


  app.databases.use(.postgres(
    hostname: Environment.get("DATABASE_HOST") ?? "localhost",
    port: Environment.get("DATABASE_PORT").flatMap(Int.
    init(_:)) ?? PostgresConfiguration.ianaPortNumber,
    username: Environment.get("DATABASE_USERNAME") ??
    "postgres",
    password: Environment.get("DATABASE_PASSWORD") ??
    "postgres",
    database: Environment.get("DATABASE_NAME") ?? "restaurantdb"
  ), as: .psql)


  app.migrations.add(CreateRestaurant())
  app.migrations.add(CreateReview())
  app.views.use(.leaf)


  // register routes
  try routes(app)
}
```

2. Proceed to **routes.swift**, and create routes as follows:

```
import Vapor


func routes(_ app: Application) throws {


    let restaurantController = RestaurantController()

    let reviewsController = ReviewsController()


    // localhost:8080/restaurant POST
    app.post("restaurant", use: restaurantController.create)


    // localhost:8080/restaurant GET
    app.get("restaurant",use: restaurantController.all)


    // localhost:8080/restaurant/:restaurantId DELETE

    app.delete("restaurant",":restaurantId", use:
    restaurantController.delete)


    // localhost:8080/reviews POST
    app.post("reviews", use: reviewsController.create)


    // localhost:8080/restaurant/:restaurantId/reviews

    app.get("restaurant",":restaurantId","reviews", use:
    reviewsController.getByRestaurantId)


}
```

3. Next, run the project and test the routes. **GET** will run perfectly fine, but as soon as you try the **POST** for the restaurant with a poster payload of more than 16 KB, you will get the error, as shown in the following figure:

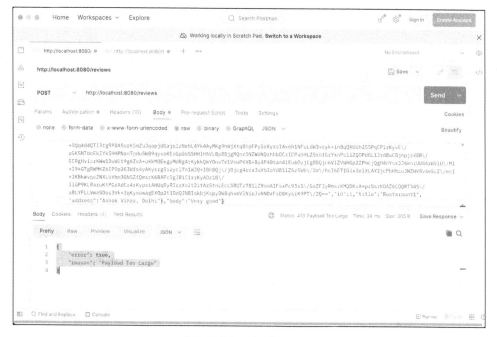

FIGURE 8.9 Payload too large.

This happened because, by default, Vapor limits streaming body collection to only 16KB in size:

- We can configure this using **app.routes** for all routes:

```
// Increases the streaming body collection limit to 500kb
app.routes.defaultMaxBodySize = "5mb"
```

- To configure the request body collection strategy for individual routes, we can use the body parameter like the following:

```
// Collects streaming bodies (up to 5mb in size) before
calling this route.

app.on(.POST, "restaurant", body: .collect(maxSize: "5mb")) {
  req in

      // Handle request.

}
```

4. Send the POST request again, and this time, it should succeed without any error.

IOS APP

Furthermore, the basics of creating an iOS project are already covered in *Chapter 6: Building User Interfaces for iOS*; therefore, we will not revisit them again here. Open Xcode, and follow the following steps:

1. Create a new iOS app project named **RestaurantApp**.

2. Check **SwiftUI** option while creating the project.

   This will create the project as shown in the following figure:

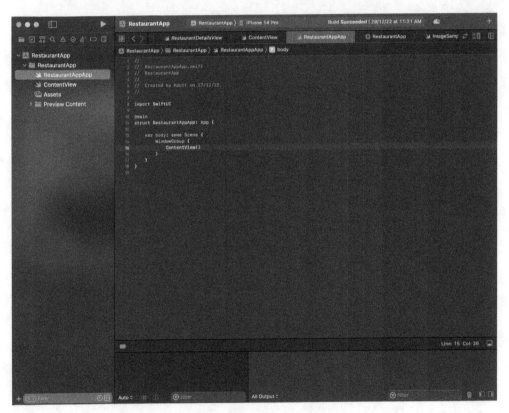

FIGURE 8.10 RestaurantApp.

Models

As in the case of the server app, let us create model classes for the client iOS app:

1. Create a new group named **Models**.

2. Create a new Swift file **Reviews.swift** for mapping **Reviews** from the server response. Create a codable struct review as follows:

```
import Foundation

struct Review: Codable {

var id: Int?

   var title: String

   var body: String

   var restaurant: Restaurant?

}
```

3. Create another Swift file **Restaurant.swift**, for mapping **Restaurant** from the server response. Similar to the previous step, create a codable struct **Restaurant** as follows:

```
import Foundation

import SwiftUI

struct Restaurant: Codable {

   var id: Int?

   var title: String

   var poster: String

   var address: String

   private enum RestaurantKeys: String, CodingKey {

      case id

      case title

      case poster
```

```swift
        case address
    }
}

extension Restaurant {
  init(from decoder: Decoder) throws {
    let container = try decoder.container(keyedBy:
    RestaurantKeys.self)
    self.id = try container.decode(Int.self, forKey: .id)
    self.title = try container.decode(String.self, forKey:
    .title)
    self.poster = try container.decode(String.self, forKey:
    .poster)
    self.address = try container.decode(String.self, forKey:
    .address)
  }


  func posterImage() -> Image? {
    guard let stringData = Data(base64Encoded: self.poster),
      let image = UIImage(data: stringData) else {
        print("Error: couldn't create UIImage")
        return nil
      }
    return Image(uiImage: image)
  }
}
```

4. After adding these model files, the new project structure will look as shown in the following figure:

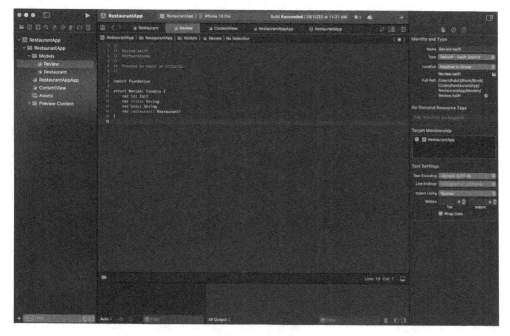

FIGURE 8.11 Models.

NETWORKING

Let us discuss the networking aspect of the iOS client app, which needs to communicate with the remote server for fetching restaurant information and reviews. For this, create another group in the project, and in that group, add a new Swift file **HTTPClient.swift**. After adding this file, the project structure will look as shown in the following figure:

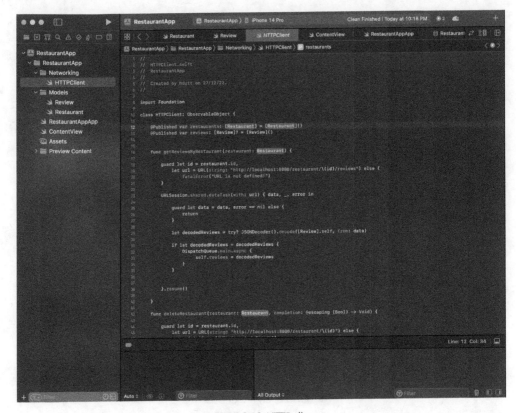

FIGURE 8.12 HTTP client.

Inside **HTTPClient.swift**, create a class **HTTPClient** conforming to the observable protocol:

1. Create two variable lists to hold **restaurants** and **reviews**:

```
class HTTPClient: ObservableObject {

    @Published var restaurants: [Restaurant] = [Restaurant]()

    @Published var reviews: [Review]? = [Review]()

}
```

2. Create a function to delete the **restaurant** from a remote server as follows:

```
func deleteRestaurant(restaurant: Restaurant, completion: @escaping (Bool) -> Void) {

    guard let id = restaurant.id,
```

```
      let url = URL(string: "http://localhost:8080/

      restaurant/\(id)") else {

        fatalError("URL is not defined!")

    }

    var request = URLRequest(url: url)

    request.httpMethod = "DELETE"

    URLSession.shared.dataTask(with: request) { data, _,

    error in

      guard let _ = data, error == nil else {

        return completion(false)

      }

      completion(true)

    }.resume()



  }
```

3. Similarly, create a function to get all **restaurants**, as follows:

```
func getAllRestaurants() {

  guard let url = URL(string: "http://localhost:8080/

  restaurant") else {

    fatalError("URL is not defined!")

  }

  URLSession.shared.dataTask(with: url) { data, response,

  error in

    guard let data = data, error == nil else {

      return

    }

    let restaurants = try? JSONDecoder().

    decode([Restaurant].self, from: data)

    if let restaurants = restaurants {
```

```
      DispatchQueue.main.async { self.restaurants = restaurants

      }

    }

  }.resume()


}
```

4. We also need the ability to create new restaurant entries in the remote database; therefore, we will create a save restaurant function as follows:

```
func saveRestaurant(name: String, poster: String, address:
String, completion: @escaping (Bool) -> Void) {

  guard let url = URL(string: "http://localhost:8080/

  restaurant") else {

    fatalError("URL is not defined!")

  }

  let restaurant = Restaurant(title: name, poster: poster,

  address: address)

  var request = URLRequest(url: url)

  request.httpMethod = "POST"

  request.addValue("application/json", forHTTPHeaderField:

  "Content-Type")

  request.httpBody = try? JSONEncoder().encode(restaurant)

  URLSession.shared.dataTask(with: request) { data,

  response, error in

    guard let _ = data, error == nil else {

      return completion(false)

    }

    completion(true)

  }.resume()

}
```

5. Next, let us get reviews for a specific restaurant by writing another function as follows:

```
func getReviewsByRestaurant(restaurant: Restaurant) {

  guard let id = restaurant.id,

    let url = URL(string: "http://localhost:8080/

    restaurant/\(id)/reviews") else {

      fatalError("URL is not defined!")

  }

  URLSession.shared.dataTask(with: url) { data, _, error in

    guard let data = data, error == nil else {

      return

    }

    let decodedReviews = try? JSONDecoder().

    decode([Review].self, from: data)

    if let decodedReviews = decodedReviews {

      DispatchQueue.main.async {

        self.reviews = decodedReviews

      }

    }

  }.resume()

}
```

6. Last but not least, we would also want to be able to add reviews for a restaurant. Let us create a function for that as follows:

```
func saveReview(review: Review, completion: @escaping (Bool) ->

Void) {

  guard let url = URL(string: "http://localhost:8080/

  reviews") else {

    fatalError("URL is not defined!")

  }

  var request = URLRequest(url: url)
```

```
request.httpMethod = "POST"

request.addValue("application/json", forHTTPHeaderField:

"Content-Type")

request.httpBody = try? JSONEncoder().encode(review)

URLSession.shared.dataTask(with: request) { data,

response, error in

  guard let _ = data, error == nil else {

    return completion(false)

  }


  completion(true)

}.resume()

}
```

USER INTERFACE

In the user interface, we need three views to visualize the data stored in the remote database. On the landing page, we would like to have a list view to showcase all restaurants fetched from the server. For this, let us create our landing page in **ContentView.swift** file using Swift UI as follows:

```
import Foundation

import SwiftUI

struct ContentView: View {

    @State private var isPresented: Bool = false

    @Environment(\.presentationMode) var presentationMode

    let screenSize = UIScreen.main.bounds

    @ObservedObject var httpClient = HTTPClient()


    var body: some View {

        NavigationView {
```

```
List(self.httpClient.restaurants, id: \.id) { restaurant in


    NavigationLink(destination: RestaurantDetails-
    View(restaurant: restaurant)) {
        VStack {
            restaurant.posterImage()?
                .resizable()
                .aspectRatio(contentMode: .fit)
            Text(restaurant.title)
                .frame(maxWidth: .infinity)
                .padding()
                .foregroundColor(Color.white)
                .background(Color.blue)
                .font(.system(size: 25))
                .cornerRadius(10)
        }
    }
}
.navigationBarTitle("Restaurant")
.navigationBarItems(trailing: Button(action: {
    self.isPresented = true
}){
    Image(systemName: "plus")
})
.onAppear {
    self.httpClient.getAllRestaurants()
}
```

```
        }.sheet(isPresented: $isPresented, onDismiss: {

            self.httpClient.getAllRestaurants()

        }, content: {

            AddRestaurantView()

        })

    }

}


struct ContentView_Previews: PreviewProvider {

    static var previews: some View {

        ContentView()

    }

}
```

This will give some compile errors due to missing classes, as highlighted in bold, namely, **AddRestaurantView** and **RestaurantDetailsView**.

Now let us discuss these classes. These classes are not present at the moment, but we will need them to visualize and add **Restaurant** flow and view **Restaurant** detail. Therefore, the next step would be to add a new file in the project, **AddRestaurantView.swift**, and add UI for the **Restaurant** flow as follows:

```
import SwiftUI

import PhotosUI

struct AddRestaurantView: View {

  @Environment(\.presentationMode) private var presentationMode

  @State private var name: String = ""

  @State private var address: String = ""

  @State private var posterPicker: PhotosPickerItem? = nil

  @State private var selectedPoster: Data? = nil
```

```
private func saveRestaurant() {

  // get the selected poster

  let posterBase64 = selectedPoster?.base64EncodedString() ?? ""

  HTTPClient().saveRestaurant(name: self.name, poster:

  posterBase64, address: address) { success in

    if success {

      // close the modal

      self.presentationMode.wrappedValue.dismiss()

    } else {

      // show user the error message that save was not successful

    }

  }

}

  private func browseImage() {

}

var body: some View {

  NavigationView {

    ScrollView {

      VStack(alignment: .center, spacing: 20) {


        TextField("Enter name", text: self.$name)

          .textFieldStyle(RoundedBorderTextFieldStyle())

        TextField("Enter Address", text: self.$address)

          .textFieldStyle(RoundedBorderTextFieldStyle())


        PhotosPicker(

          selection: $posterPicker,
```

```swift
            matching: .images,
            photoLibrary: .shared()) {
                Text("Select Poster")
            }
            .onChange(of: posterPicker) { newItem in
                Task {
                    // Retrive selected asset in the
                    form of Data
                    if let data = try? await newItem?.
                    loadTransferable(type: Data.self) {
                        selectedPoster = data
                    }
                }
            }
        if let selectedPoster,
           let uiImage = UIImage(data: selectedPoster) {
                Image(uiImage: uiImage)
                    .resizable()
                    .scaledToFit()
                    .frame(width: 250, height: 250)
        }
        Button("Add Restaraunt") {
            // save the movie
            self.saveRestaurant()
        }
        .padding(8)
        .foregroundColor(Color.white)
```

```
        .background(Color.green)

        .cornerRadius(8)

    }.padding()

        .background(Color.black)

    }

    .navigationBarTitle("Add Restaurant")

    .navigationBarItems(trailing: Button("Close") {

      print("closed fired")

      self.presentationMode.wrappedValue.dismiss()

    })

    }

  }

}


struct AddMovieView_Previews: PreviewProvider {

  static var previews: some View {

    AddRestaurantView()

  }

}
```

Similarly, add a new file in the project, **RestaurantDetailsView. swift**, add UI for the **Restaurant** detail's view, and add a review flow as follows:

```
import SwiftUI


struct RestaurantDetailsView: View {

  let restaurant: Restaurant

  @State private var reviewTitle: String = ""

  @State private var reviewBody: String = ""
```

```swift
@ObservedObject private var httpClient = HTTPClient()

@Environment(\.presentationMode) private var presentationMode

private func deleteRestaurant() {

  HTTPClient().deleteRestaurant(restaurant: restaurant) { success in

    DispatchQueue.main.async {

      self.presentationMode.wrappedValue.dismiss()

    }

  }

}


private func saveReview() {

  let review = Review(title: self.reviewTitle, body: self.

    reviewBody, restaurant: restaurant)

    HTTPClient().saveReview(review: review) { success in

      if success {

        // load all the reviews again

        self.httpClient.getReviewsByRestaurant(restaurant:

        restaurant)

      }

    }

  }

  var body: some View {

    Form {

      restaurant.posterImage()?

        .resizable()

        .aspectRatio(contentMode: .fit)

        .padding()
```

```
Section(header: Text("ADD A REVIEW").fontWeight(.bold)) {

  VStack(alignment: .center, spacing: 10) {

    TextField("Enter Title",text: $reviewTitle)

      .textFieldStyle(RoundedBorderTextFieldStyle())


    TextField("Enter Body",text: $reviewBody)

    .textFieldStyle(RoundedBorderTextFieldStyle())

    Button("Save") {

      self.saveReview()

    }

    .frame(maxWidth: .infinity)

    .padding(10)

    .foregroundColor(Color.white)

    .background(Color.blue)

    .cornerRadius(6.0)

    .buttonStyle(PlainButtonStyle())

  }

}

Section(header: Text("REVIEWS").fontWeight(.bold)) {

  ForEach(self.httpClient.reviews ?? [Review](), id: \.id)

  { review in

    Text(review.title)

  }

}

}
```

```
        .onAppear(perform: {

          // get reviews for restaurant

          self.httpClient.getReviewsByRestaurant(restaurant:

          restaurant)

        })


        .navigationBarTitle(restaurant.title)


        .navigationBarItems(trailing: Button(action: {

          self.deleteRestaurant()

        }) {

          Image(systemName: "trash.fill")

        })

    }

}


struct RestaurantDetailsView_Previews: PreviewProvider {

    static var previews: some View {

// base64ImageSmaple1 is a base64 encoded string for a sample image

      RestaurantDetailsView(restaurant: Restaurant(title:
      "IndieKitchen", poster: base64ImageSmaple1, address: "Ashok
      Vihar Delhi"))

    }

}
```

With this, we are ready with our iOS app to communicate with the backend
server.

TEST RUN

As our database, server, and iOS app are ready, let us run the server on the local host and run the iOS app in the simulator. As soon as the app opens, it will open the landing page designed in `ContentView.swift` in the iOS project, as shown in the following figure:

FIGURE 8.13 Restaurant app landing page.

As we already have a sample **Restaurant** entry in a remote database, the iOS app fetched the details and showed them on the landing page. Next, if you click on the **+** button at the top right corner, it will arrive at the UI designed in `AddRestaurantView.swift`, as shown in the following figure:

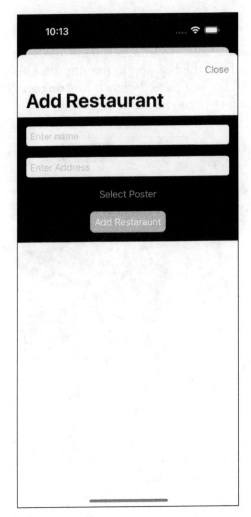

FIGURE 8.14 Add restaurant.

The **Select Poster** button, when pressed, will open the photo picker window to select an image from the stored photos on the iPhone. The **Add Restaurant** button will add a new restaurant entry to the remote database through remote server APIs.

On clicking on the **Close** button in the top right corner, the app will again go back to the restaurant list, as shown in *Figure 8.13*. On clicking on the restaurant cell view in the list, a detail's view will open, as shown in the following figure:

FIGURE 8.15 Restaurant details page.

At this point, you can see that it has already saved sample reviews. You can also add new reviews on this page.

Excellent! After all this hard work, we have finally created a working full-stack sample project and achieved our objective.

CONCLUSION

In this chapter, we practically applied the knowledge gained from all the other chapters in this book. In this chapter, we actually created and successfully completed a full-stack project with a persistent remote database layer. With this chapter, we achieved our objective of executing a full-stack iOS project with the help of Swift Vapor on the server side and Swift on the iOS client side.

In the following chapters, we will touch upon some advanced topics relating to iOS and Vapor, as well as the deployment of server and client apps.

9

ADVANCED FULL-STACK CONCEPTS

INTRODUCTION

In the previous chapter, we implemented our full-stack project. In this chapter, we will extend our understanding of the full-stack concept to some more advanced topics.

STRUCTURE

In this chapter, we will discuss the following topics:

- Middleware
- WebSocket
- APNS
- Security

OBJECTIVES

In the previous chapter, we implemented our full-stack project, but that was only at the POC level. In this chapter, we will explore some advanced topics related to full-stack, which are very important with regard to overall system design and system architecture. These concepts are a must for commercial application development.

MIDDLEWARE

Middleware is a logic chain connecting the client and a route handler to perform operations on incoming requests and outgoing responses before the request reaches the route handler and before the response reaches the client.

In a real-world application, we often need to integrate some custom logic into the request pipeline. Implementing middleware is the most common mechanism for accomplishing this. Using middleware, we can perform tasks like the following:

- Logging incoming requests.
- Catch and display errors and messages.
- Rate-limit traffic to routes.

A middleware instance is a logical layer sitting in between the router and the client that enables us to view and perform mutations on incoming requests before they reach the controllers. A middleware instance may return early or choose to forward the request to the next responder. The last responder in the chain is always the router.

Middleware can be registered globally using **app.middleware** is as follows:

```
app.middleware.use(CustomMiddleware())
```

Using route groups, it can also be added to individual routes as follows:

```
let group = app.grouped(CustomMiddleware())

group.get("someRoute") { req in

  // This request has passed through CustomMiddleware.

}
```

The order for adding middleware is important, as incoming requests will be processed in the middleware in the order they were added. Similarly, responses will also be processed in the middleware in reverse order. Application middleware always takes precedence over route-specific middleware.

Vapor adds default middleware automatically, but if we want to add a middleware before the default middleware, we can prepend the middleware as well:

```
app.middleware.use(customMiddleware, at: .beginning)
```

Creating Middleware

A few useful middlewares are shipped with Vapor, but as discussed, we might need to create our own custom middleware as per the requirements of the application. The classic example would be to create middleware to prevent users without admin rights from accessing a group of routes.

Middleware must conform to the middleware or **asyncmiddleware** protocol. After that, they are inserted into the responder chain and can be used to access and manipulate an incoming request before it reaches a route handler and access and manipulate an outgoing response before it is returned.

For example, let us create a middleware to allow access to the user only if they are an admin.

```
import Vapor


struct AdministratorMiddleware: Middleware {

  func respond(to request: Request, chainingTo next: Responder) ->
  EventLoopFuture<Response> {

    guard let adminUser = request.auth.get(User.self),
    adminUser.role == .admin else {

      return request.eventLoop.future(error: Abort(.unauthorized))

    }

    return next.respond(to: request)

  }

}
```

At this point, the user is another model we need to create and maintain in a persistent database. If we are using async/await, we can write our middleware as follows:

```
import Vapor


struct AdministratorMiddleware: AsyncMiddleware {

  func respond(to request: Request, chainingTo next: AsyncResponder)
  async throws -> Response {
```

```
guard let adminUser = request.auth.get(User.self), adminUser.
role == .admin else {

    throw Abort(.unauthorized)

}

return try await next.respond(to: request)

}

}
```

Another example would be to modify the response by adding a custom header. We can create a middleware for this as follows:

```
import Vapor


struct VersionHeaderMiddleware: Middleware {

  func respond(to request: Request, chainingTo next: Responder) ->
  EventLoopFuture<Response> {

    next.respond(to: request).map { response in

      response.headers.add(name: "Version", value: "v2.5")

      return response

    }

  }

}
```

This middleware will add an app version to the header and can wait till the response is received from the responder chain before manipulating the response.

Similar to the previous example, if we are using async/await, we can write our middleware as follows:

```
import Vapor


struct VersionHeaderMiddleware: AsyncMiddleware {
```

```
func respond(to request: Request, chainingTo next: AsyncResponder)
async throws -> Response {

   let response = try await next.respond(to: request)
   response.headers.add(name: "Version", value: "v2.5")
   return response

}

}
```

WEBSOCKETS

There are certain scenarios where the server needs to send information to the client app rather than the client app requesting information from the server. WebSockets allow two-way communication between a client and server, unlike HTTP's request and response pattern. WebSocket implements a peer structure where peers can communicate and send an arbitrary number of messages in both directions. The WebSocket API provided by Vapor allows us to implement a mechanism where clients and servers can both handle messages asynchronously.

WebSocket endpoints can be easily added to the existing Vapor application using the Routing API. We just need to use the WebSocket method, like the get or post methods:

```
app.webSocket("restaurantSocket") { request, websocket in

   //Connected WebSocket

   print(websocket)

}
```

WebSocket routes can be grouped and protected by middleware, similar to normal routes. WebSocket handlers accept the newly established WebSocket connection in addition to the incoming HTTP request.

Messages

The WebSocket class has methods for receiving and sending messages, as well as listening to events. WebSockets can transmit data using two protocols, that is, text and binary. Text messages are treated as UTF-8 strings, whereas binary data is interpreted as a byte array.

Sending

For sending messages, we can use WebSocket's **send** method:

```
websocket.send("Hello World")
```

This method sends a text message to the other side. For sending binary messages, we can send them by passing a **[UInt8]**.

The message-sending process is asynchronous. Notifying that the message has finished sending or failed, we can supply an **EventLoopPromise** to the sender:

```
let promise = eventLoop.makePromise(of: Void.self)

websocket.send(...., promise: promise)

promise.futureResult.whenComplete { result in

  // Success or failure.

}
```

By using async/await, we can await the result:

```
let result = try await websocket.send(...)
```

Receiving

Incoming messages are handled with the **onText** and **onBinary** callbacks:

```
websocket.onText { websocket, text in

  // String received by WebSocket.

  print(text)

}


websocket.onBinary { websocket, binary in

  // Bytes received by WebSocket.

  print(binary)

}
```

The WebSocket is the first parameter in these callbacks to prevent reference cycles. For taking any action on the **Websocket** after receiving the data, use this reference. For example, we can send a reply as follows:

```
// Echoes received messages.

websocket.onText { websocket, text in

  websocket.send(text)

}
```

Closing

To close a WebSocket, we just need to call the **close** method:

```
websocket.close()
```

This method returns a future that will be completed when the WebSocket has closed. Like the send method, we can also pass a promise to this method as follows:

```
websocket.close(promise: nil)
```

And for using async/await:

```
try await websocket.close()
```

For notification when the peer closes the connection, use the **onClose** method. The future will be completed if either the client or server closes the WebSocket.

```
websocket.onClose.whenComplete { result in

  // Success or failure to close.

}
```

The **closeCode** property gets set when the WebSocket closes:

APNS

Vapor's **Apple Push Notification Service** (**APNS**) APIs, built on top of **APNSwift** (*https://github.com/kylebrowning/APNSwift*), make it easy to authenticate and send push notifications to Apple devices.

To start with using APNS, first add the package to the dependencies in **Package. swift**:

```
let package = Package(

  name: "Restaurant-Server",

  dependencies: [

      // Other dependencies here...

    .package(url: "https://github.com/vapor/apns.git", from: "3.0.0"),

  ],


  targets: [

    .target(name: "App", dependencies: [

      // Other dependencies here...

      .product(name: "APNS", package: "apns")

    ]),

    // Other targets here...

  ]

)
```

After editing the manifest directly, it will automatically fetch the new dependency. However, if it does not happen, open the Terminal app and run swift package resolve to fetch the new dependency.

After adding the APNS module, a new property **apns** will be added to the application. To send push notifications, we first need to set the configuration property with our credentials to the following:

```
import APNS


// Configure APNS with JWT authentication.

app.apns.configuration = try .init(

  let pathToP8File = "<#path to .p8 file#>"
```

```
let keyIdentifier = "<#key identifier#>"

let teamIdentifier = "<#team identifier#>"

authenticationMethod: .jwt(

  key: .private(filePath:),

  keyIdentifier: keyIdentifier,

  teamIdentifier: teamIdentifier

),


  topic: "<#topic#>",

  environment: .sandbox

)


//Configure APNS with TLS based auth.

app.apns.configuration = try .init(

  let privateKeyPath = "<#path to private key#>"

  let pemPath = "<#path to pem file#>"

  let pemPassword = "<#pem password#>"


  authenticationMethod: .tls(

  privateKeyPath: privateKeyPath,

  pemPath: pemPath,

  pemPassword: pemPassword

  ),

  topic: "<#topic#>",

  environment: .sandbox

)
```

Once we are done with the APNS configuration, we can push notifications using **apns.send** method:

```
// Send push notification.
try app.apns.send(
    .init(title: "Notification", subtitle: "This is a test push
    notification"),
    to: "Device Token"
).wait()
// Or
try await app.apns.send(
    .init(title: "Notification", subtitle: "This is a test push
    notification"),
    to: "Device Token"
)
```

Always use **req.apns** when inside a route handler:

```
// Send push notification.
app.get("test-push") { req -> EventLoopFuture<HTTPStatus> in
    req.apns.send(.init(title: "Notification", subtitle: "This is a
    test push notification"),
    to: "Device Token")
    .map { .ok }
}


// Or
app.get("test-push") { req async throws -> HTTPStatus in
    try await req.apns.send(.init(title: "Notification", subtitle:
    "This is a test push notification"),
    to: "Device Token")
    return .ok
}
```

The first parameter in the **send** method is the push notification alert, and the second parameter is the **target** device token.

APNSwiftAlert is the metadata for the push notification alert. More details can be checked here *(https://developer.apple.com/library/archive/ documentation/NetworkingInternet/Conceptual/RemoteNotificationsPG/ PayloadKeyReference. html)*:

```
let alert = APNSwiftAlert(

  title: "Alert Title",

  subtitle: "Test Push",

  body: "Test Push body"

)
```

The **APNSwiftAlert** type can be passed to the **send** method, and it will automatically wrap in an **APNSwiftPayload**.

APNSwiftPayload is the actual metadata of the push notification, such as the alert, badge count, and so on. More details can be found here *(https://developer.apple.com/library/archive/documentation/Networking Internet/Conceptual/RemoteNotificationsPG/PayloadKeyReference.html)*:

```
let payload = APNSwiftPayload(alert: alert, badge: 1,
sound: .normal("test.wav"))
```

This payload can be passed to the **send** method. Apple also provides the ability to add custom payload data to each notification using **APNSwiftNotification**:

```
struct CustomNotification: APNSwiftNotification {

  let custom: [String]

  let payload: APNSwiftPayload


  init(custom: [String], payload: APNSwiftPayload) {

    self.custom = custom

    self. payload = payload

  }

}
```

```
let payload: APNSwiftPayload = APNSwiftPayload(alert: alert, badge: 1,
sound: .normal("test.wav"))

let notification = CustomNotification(custom: ["test1", "test2"],
payload: payload)
```

This custom notification can be passed to the send method.

SECURITY

Security is the most important aspect of any application. Without security implementation, an app cannot be released to the public; otherwise, it will be a Pandora's Box of problems. On the server side, the most important aspect of security is Authentication. On the client side, too, there is a need to store sensitive data like passwords securely. For securing sensitive data on iOS, we will study Keychains in this section.

Authentication

Authentication is done to establish a user's identity. This can be done through the verification of credentials such as a username and password or a unique token. Authentication is different from authorization, as the latter is the act of verifying a user's permissions to perform certain app flows.

Vapor's Authentication API supports authentication using Basic and **Bearer** in the **Authorization** header. It also supports authentication through the data decoded from the **Content** API.

For using the **Authentication** API, first we need a **User** type conforming to the Authenticatable protocol. **User** type can be a struct, class, or **Fluent Model**. In the following examples, let us create a **User** struct that has one **property: userName**:

```
import Vapor


struct User: Authenticatable {

  var userName: String

}
```

In the following example, we will use an instance of an authenticator middleware named **UserAuthenticatorMiddleware**:

```
let protected = app.grouped(UserAuthenticatorMiddleware())

protected.get("user") { req -> String in

  try req.auth.require(User.self).userName

}
```

req.auth.require will fetch the authenticated **User**. This method will throw an error if authentication fails.

Basic Authentication

Basic authentication sends a username and password concatenated with a colon, like **user:secret**, base-64 encoded, and prefixed with **Basic** in the **Authorization** header.

```
GET /me HTTP/1.1

Authorization: Basic dXNlcjpzZWNyZXQ=
```

Basic authentication is generally used once while logging a user into the system and generating a token. This minimizes the frequency of exposing the user's sensitive password. Basic authorization should never be sent as plaintext or an unverified TLS connection.

To implement **Basic** authentication in the app, we will create a new authenticator conforming to **BasicAuthenticator**. Let us look at the example as follows:

```
import Vapor

struct UserAuthenticatorMiddleware: BasicAuthenticator {

  func authenticate(

    basic: BasicAuthorization,

    for request: Request

  ) -> EventLoopFuture<Void> {
```

```
        if basic.username == "username" && basic.password == "password" {

            request.auth.login(App.User(name: basic.username))

        }

        return request.eventLoop.makeSucceededFuture(())

    }

}
```

If we are using async/await, we can use **AsyncBearerAuthenticator**
as follows:

```
import Vapor


struct UserAuthenticatorMiddleware: AsyncBasicAuthenticator {

    func authenticate(

        basic: BasicAuthorization,

        for request: Request

    ) async throws {

        if basic.username == "username" && basic.password == "password" {

            request.auth.login(User(name: App.User(name: basic.username)))

        }

    }

}
```

The **BasicAuthenticator** protocol requires us to implement the
authenticate(basic:for:) function, which gets invoked when
an incoming request contains the Authorization: **Basic** header. A
BasicAuthorization struct incapsulating the username and password is
passed to this method.

In the preceding example, the authenticator uses hard-coded values to test
for the username and password. In a real authenticator, we will check against
a database entry or an external API. Precisely due to this, the **authenticate** method allows us to return to the future.

NOTE *We should never store passwords in a database as plaintext. The best practice is to always use password hashes for future comparisons.*

If the authentication parameters are correct (in the preceding example, they match the hard-coded values), the **User** is logged in. If the authentication parameters do not match, authentication fails, and the user is not logged in.

Bearer Authentication

Bearer authentication works by sending a token prefixed with **Bearer** in the Authorization header. The following is an example:

```
GET /me HTTP/1.1

Authorization: Bearer token
```

Bearer authentication is generally used for the authentication of API endpoints. The user requests a Bearer token by sending credentials such as a username and password to a login endpoint. This token has an expiration timeline based on the application's needs.

While the token is valid, the user can use it instead of using credentials to authenticate. When the token expires, a new token can be generated using the login endpoint.

For implementing **Bearer** authentication in the app, create a new authenticator conforming to the **BearerAuthenticator** protocol. The following is an example of an authenticator to verify the request:

```
import Vapor

struct UserAuthenticatorMiddleware: BearerAuthenticator {

  func authenticate(

    bearer: BearerAuthorization,

    for request: Request

  ) -> EventLoopFuture<Void> {

    if bearer.token == "token" {

      request.auth.login(App.User(name: "HardCodedUser"))

    }

    return request.eventLoop.makeSucceededFuture(())
```

```
  }

}
```

If we are using async/await, we can use **AsyncBearerAuthenticator** as follows:

```
import Vapor

struct UserAuthenticator: AsyncBearerAuthenticator {
  func authenticate(
    bearer: BearerAuthorization,
    for request: Request
  ) async throws {

    if bearer.token == "token" {

      request.auth.login(App.User(name: "HardCodedUser"))

    }

  }

}
```

BearerAuthenticator protocol requires us to implement **authenticate(bearer:for:)**, which gets invoked when an incoming request contains the **Authorization: Bearer** header. A **BearerAuthorization** struct having the token is passed to this method.

In the preceding example of an authenticator, the token is tested against a hard-coded value. In the real world, though, we will verify the token by checking against a database entry or using cryptographic measures, as done with JWT. Due to this, the authenticate method allows us to return to the future.

If the authentication parameters are correct (in our example, match the hard-coded value), a **User** named **HardCodedUser** will be logged in. If the authentication parameters do not match, the user will not log in, and thus, authentication will fail.

Composition

Multiple authenticators can also be combined together to create much more complex endpoint authentication. As authenticator middleware will not reject the request in case authentication fails, more than one middleware can be chained with each other.

For the same user type, authenticators can be composed by chaining more than one authenticator. Let us take an example:

```
app.grouped(UserPasswordAuthenticator())

  .grouped(UserTokenAuthenticator())

  .grouped(User.guardMiddleware())

  .post("loginUser")

{ req in

  let authenticatedUser = try req.auth.require(User.self)

  // Do something with authenticated user...

}
```

In the preceding example, two authenticators, **UserPassword Authenticator** and **UserTokenAuthenticator**, are added to the route group, and **GuardMiddleware** is chained after the authenticators to require that the **User** be successfully authenticated.

This composition results in a sort of hybrid route access where the route can be accessed by password as well as by token. Hence, this route allows a user to login and generate a token, which can be reused to generate new tokens.

Another way to compose authentication is by chaining authenticators, but for different user types. Let us look at the following example:

```
app.grouped(AdminAuthenticator())

  .grouped(UserAuthenticatorMiddleware())

  .get("secure")

{ req in

  guard req.auth.has(Admin.self) || req.auth.has(User.self) else {

    throw Abort(.unauthorized)

  }

  // Do something here.

}
```

The preceding example assumes that after adding **AdminAuthenticator** and **UserAuthenticatorMiddleware** authenticators to the route group, they authenticate **Admin** and **User**, respectively. In place of using **GuardMiddleware**, a check in the route handler is added to check if the **Admin** or **User** are authenticated. Otherwise, an error is thrown.

This composition results in a route that can be accessed by two different types of users with possibly different methods of authentication. Such routes allow for normal user authentication while still giving access to an admin user.

Session

Vapor's Session API provides the capability to automatically persist user authentication between requests as it stores a unique identifier for the user in the request's session data after user login. For subsequent requests, the user's identifier is fetched from the session and is used to authenticate the user before calling the route handler.

Sessions are advised for front-end Web applications that serve HTML directly to Web browsers, whereas for APIs, stateless and token-based authentication are recommended.

To use session-based authentication, we first need a type conforming to **SessionAuthenticatable**. For example:

```
struct User {

  var eMail: String

}
```

Conforming to **SessionAuthenticatable**, we need to specify a **sessionID**, which will be stored in the session data and must be a unique identifier for the user:

```
extension User: SessionAuthenticatable {

  var sessionId: String {

    self.eMail

  }

}
```

For simplicity, in the preceding example, the **User** type will use the e-mail address as the unique identifier.

Next, we need a **SessionAuthenticator** for resolving instances of **User** from the persistent session identifier as follows:

```
struct UserSessionAuthenticator: SessionAuthenticator {

  func authenticate(sessionID: String, for request: Request) ->
  EventLoopFuture<Void> {

    let user = App.User(eMail: sessionID)

    request.auth.login(user)

    return request.eventLoop.makeSucceededFuture(())

  }

}
```

While using async/await, use the **AsyncSessionAuthenticator** as follows:

```
struct UserSessionAuthenticator: AsyncSessionAuthenticator {

  func authenticate(sessionID: String, for request: Request) async
  throws {

    let user = App.User(eMail: sessionID)

    request.auth.login(user)

  }

}
```

In our example, all the information needed to initialize **User** is contained in the session identifier, which will not hold true in the real world. In the real world, most likely, we will use the session identifier to perform a database or API request to fetch the user data before authentication.

Let us create a simple bearer authenticator in our example to perform the initial authentication as follows:

```
struct UserBearerAuthenticator: AsyncBearerAuthenticator {

  func authenticate(bearer: BearerAuthorization, for request: Request)
  async throws {
```

```
if bearer.token == "test token" {

    let user = User(email: "examplemail@somedomain.com")

    request.auth.login(user)

    }

  }

}
```

This authenticator will authenticate the user with the email **examplemail@ somedomain.com** when the bearer token test is sent.

At last, let us integrate all these pieces together in the application:

1. Create a route group which requires user auth.

```
let protectedGroup = app.routes.grouped([
app.sessions.middleware,
UserSessionAuthenticator(),
UserBearerAuthenticator(),
User.guardMiddleware(),
  ])
```

2. Add **GET /email** route for reading the email address of the user:

```
protected.get("email") { req -> String in
   try req.auth.require(User.self).eMail
   }
```

SessionsMiddleware is added to enable session support on the application. The **SessionAuthenticator** is added next to handle authenticating the user in an active session.

If, in the session, authentication has not persisted yet, the request will be forwarded to the **UserBearerAuthenticator**, which will check the bearer token for authenticating the user.

Finally, **guardMiddleware()** makes sure that the user has been authenticated by one of the previous middleware; otherwise, an error will be thrown.

JWT

JWT provides **JWTAuthenticator** to authenticate JSON Web Tokens in incoming requests. First, create a new type conforming to **JWTPayload** as follows:

```
struct JWTSessionToken: Content, Authenticatable, JWTPayload {

  let expireTime: TimeInterval = 60 * 30

  var expirationClaim: ExpirationClaim

  var userId: UUID

  init(userId: UUID) {

    self.userId = userId

    self.expirationClaim = ExpirationClaim(value: Date().
    addingTimeInterval(expireTime))

  }

  init(user: User) throws {

    self.userId = try user.requireID()

    self.expirationClaim = ExpirationClaim(value: Date().
    addingTimeInterval(expireTime))

  }

  func verify(using signer: JWTSigner) throws {
    try expirationClaim.verifyNotExpired()

  }

}
```

Next, we define a struct for the data encapsulated in a successful login response. For the sake of simplicity, the response in the example only has one property, which is a string representing a signed JWT:

```
struct JWTTokenReponse: Content {

  var jwtToken: String

}
```

Using our model for the JWT token and response, we can use a password-protected login route to return a **JWTTokenReponse**, which includes a signed **JWTSessionToken** shown as follows:

```
let passProtected = app.grouped(User.authenticator(), User.
guardMiddleware())
```

```
passProtected.post("login") { req -> JWTTokenReponse in
    let user = try req.auth.require(User.self)
    let payload = try JWTSessionToken (with: user)
    return JWTTokenReponse(jwtToken: try req.jwt.sign(payload))

}
```

Conversely, if you do not want to use an authenticator, follow the following code:

```
app.post("login") { req -> JWTTokenReponse in

    // Validate credential and get userId for provided user

    let payload = try JWTSessionToken(userId: userId)

    return JWTTokenReponse(jwtToken: try req.jwt.sign(payload))

}
```

After conforming the payload to **Authenticatable** and **JWTPayload**, we can actually generate a route authenticator using the authenticator method, which can be added to a route group for automatically fetching and verifying the JWT before the route is called:

```
let secure = app.grouped(JWTSessionToken.authenticator(),
JWTSessionToken. guardMiddleware())
```

At this point, the guard middleware will require that authorization to succeed. We can access the authenticated JWT payload using **req.auth** inside the protected routes:

```
secure.post("validateLoggedUser") { req -> HTTPStatus in

    let jwtsessionToken = try req.auth.require(JWTSessionToken.self)
    print(jwtsessionToken.userId)
    return .ok

}
```

KeyChain

Similar to servers, the most important aspect of software development on the client side also happens to be application security. Users expect that their applications will keep their information private and protect the information from potential threats.

In this section, we will dive into the basics of iOS security. We will work with the iOS keychain to keep users' data private and protected.

Keychains are one of the most important security elements for Apple developers. It is a specialized database for storing metadata and sensitive information. For storing small critical data such as secrets and passwords, using Keychain is the best practice.

Security is a difficult and specialized stream of engineering; therefore, attempting your own custom solution is a bad idea. Even if your app is not for a strategic or financial institution, storing private user data should not be taken lightly; otherwise, you may encounter legal complications in addition to hacker attacks.

The keychain is not limited to passwords. We can store other secrets that are critical for users, such as credit card information. We can also store cryptographic keys and certificates that we manage with certificate, key, and trust services, which enable the user to engage in secure communications and to establish trust with other users and devices.

When we want to store a secret, like a password or cryptographic key, we package it as a keychain item. Along with the data itself, we provide a set of publicly visible attributes to control the item's accessibility and make it searchable. Authorized processes can use keychain services to find the item and decrypt its data.

Adding a Password to Keychain

Let us take this example. First, define a structure that will hold the credentials:

```
struct Credentials {

  var userName: String

  var password: String

}
```

Next, define error enumeration, which can be used to communicate keychain access errors:

```
enum KeychainError: Error {

  case noPassword

  case unexpectedPasswordData
```

```
    case unhandledError(status: OSStatus)

}
```

Identify the server that the app is working with:

```
static let server = "www.hemdutt.com"
```

Use an instance of the credentials structure and the server constant to create an add query:

```
let account = credentials.userName

let password = credentials.password.data(using: String.Encoding.utf8)!
var query: [String: Any] = [kSecClass as String: kSecClassInternetPassword,
                    kSecAttrAccount as String: account,
                    kSecAttrServer as String: server,
                    kSecValueData as String: password]
```

At this point, the first key-value pair indicates that the item is an Internet password; from here, keychain services infer that the data is secret and requires encryption. This is also to ensure that the item has attributes to distinguish itself from other Internet passwords. The next two key-value pairs in the query provide this information by attaching the username as the account, along with a domain name to this password as the server:

```
With the query complete, we can simply feed this to the
SecItemAdd(_:_:) function:

let status = SecItemAdd(query as CFDictionary, nil)

guard status == errSecSuccess else {

  throw KeychainError.unhandledError(status: status)

}
```

Although we can ignore the return data supplied by reference in the second argument of an add operation, always check the function's return status to ensure that the operation succeeds.

To be able to find the item later, we can rely on our knowledge of its attributes. In our example, the server and the account are distinguishing characteristics of the item. As long as the app never adds similar items with varying attributes, like passwords for different accounts on the same server, we can omit these dynamic attributes as search parameters and rather retrieve them along with the item.

If the app does add items with varying dynamic attributes, we will need to choose among them during retrieval. It may make sense to further characterize the item by adding more attributes.

CONCLUSION

In this chapter, we covered some advanced topics related to full-stack, which are very important with respect to the overall system design and system architecture. Concepts like Middleware, WebSocket, APNS, and Security are integral to any real-world software system development. This chapter should be treated as a launchpad for a deep dive into these concepts and to understand the software system holistically.

In the upcoming chapter, we will discuss deployment processes for server-side and iOS apps.

CHAPTER 10

DEPLOYING iOS AND VAPOR APPLICATIONS

INTRODUCTION

We are done building our awesome Vapor server app and iOS app. However, these are still with us, and we definitely want to showcase them to the world. Here comes our next challenge, which is deploying these applications for the world and letting the world have a taste of our full-stack application system.

There are lots of different ways to deploy our vapor application, and we will study a few of these in this chapter. On the other side, iOS only has one way to deploy and release apps to the public, and that is through the App Store. We will study this as well in this chapter.

STRUCTURE

In this chapter, we will discuss the following topics:

- Vapor app deployment
  - Heroku
  - Docker
- iOS app store release

OBJECTIVES

The objective of this chapter is to study and understand the deployment process(es) for our iOS and Vapor apps to the public. For Vapor apps, we will study deployment through Heroku and Docker, whereas for iOS, there is only one way, and that is through the App Store, which will also be covered in this chapter.

VAPOR APP DEPLOYMENT

There are lots of different ways to deploy our application, and one of them is through Heroku.

Heroku

Heroku is a **Platform as a Service** (**PaaS**) that will handle arranging TLS and viewing application logs, traffic monitoring, and much more.

To deploy your app through Heroku, first sign up at *https://signup.heroku. com/*, as shown in the following figure:

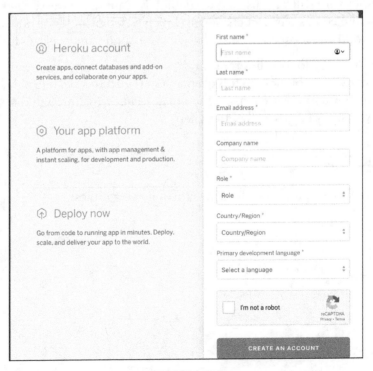

FIGURE 10.1 Sign up.

1. Install the Heroku CLI tool using the following command:

   ```
   brew install heroku/brew/heroku
   ```

2. Log in to *Heroku* in the terminal and follow the instructions:

   ```
   heroku login
   ```

3. Navigate to the dashboard and create a new app, as shown in the following figure:

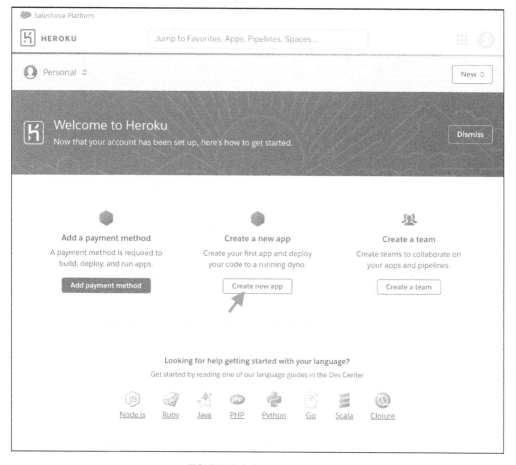

FIGURE 10.2 Create a new app.

4. Once you click on **Create new app**, you will arrive at another page where you can start the process of giving details about your app, as shown in the following figure:

FIGURE 10.3 App details.

The name of the app will be the subdomain where the app can be reached.

5. Next, we will connect our Heroku application to our local git repository by running the following command in the terminal.

```
$ heroku git:remote -a Restaurant-Server
```

6. Now that we are connected, we need to create a **Procfile**. The **Procfile** is used by Heroku to know how to run our app. To create a **Procfile**, open the terminal and enter the following command:

```
$ touch Procfile
```

We need our Procfile to look like **web: Run serve --env production --hostname 0.0.0.0 --port $PORT**:

```
$ echo "web: Run serve --env production" \
"--hostname 0.0.0.0 --port \$PORT" > Procfile
```

In our case, it is a Web process because we want to expose our application using HTTP to the outside world.

After **Web:** we need to define the command that Heroku should execute to launch our application. We want to start our Run executable defined in our **Package.swift** file and want to serve our application. We want to run our app in a production environment. Next, we define the hostname, and finally, we define the port we want to bind to. While running the app with Xcode, it automatically binds to port **8080**. However, the port Heroku decides can vary and is not guaranteed to be **8080**. Due to this, Heroku provides a **PORT** environment variable that can be used to bind to.

Add this file to the git repository:

```
$ git add Procfile

$ git commit -m "Procfile added"
```

We are all set to deploy our application. Open the terminal and run the following command:

```
git push heroku master
```

You might face which states Heroku was unable to detect your **buildpack**. There is a Heroku **buildpack** for Vapor (*https://github.com/vapor-community/heroku-buildpack*) maintained by some contributors. We can add this **buildpack** to our application by running

```
heroku buildpacks:set vapor/vapor
```

Furthermore, start building the application.

```
$ git push heroku master
```

This can take a while, and after that, you should get the message that your application has been deployed.

```
"https://restaurantserver.herokuapp.com/ is deployed to Heroku"
```

Therefore, we can hit the URL and check out our app in action.

To add a simple Postgres database to our application, we will again open a terminal and run the following command:

```
$ heroku addons:create heroku-postgresql:restaurantdb
```

We now have to tell our app how to access the database. In the **app** directory, run the following:

```
heroku config
```

This will output something like the following:

```
DATABASE_URL: postgres://someURL:5432/dfr80mvoo550b4
```

DATABASE_URL here represents our **postgres** database.

NOTE *We should never hard code the static URL from this as Heroku will change it, and that will break our application.*

You should always read the environment variable at runtime:

```
guard let databaseURL = Environment.get("DATABASE_URL") else { return }


//Connect with database as

var postgresDbConfig = PostgresConfiguration(url: databaseURL)
postgresDbConfig.tlsConfiguration = .makeClientConfiguration()
postgresDbConfig.tlsConfiguration?.certificateVerification = .none
app.databases.use(.postgres(configuration: postgresDbConfig), as: .psql)
```

Docker

Most developers writing server-side Vapor applications are from iOS or macOS backgrounds. That is why their development environment is macOS, but the vast majority of servers run on Linux. While developing Web apps with Vapor, we have to make sure this difference does not cause issues while deploying our app.

To work around this problem, we can use containerization. For containerization, we can use Docker, which is the most popular containerization tool. Using Docker in the development phase, we can rest assured that what runs in the local image of our app will run on the server.

Using Docker to deploy the Vapor app has multiple benefits, as follows:

- The Dockerized app can be spun up reliably with a Docker daemon using the same commands on any platform.

- We can orchestrate multiple services that are needed for a full deployment using Docker Composer or Kubernetes manifests.

- It is easy to test an app's horizontal scalability on the development machine.

In this section, we will explore how to deploy our Dockerized app on a server. The simplest deployment would involve installing Docker on the server and running the same commands as on your development machine to spin up the application.

More complicated and robust deployments would differ depending on the hosting solution. Solutions like AWS provide built-in support for Kubernetes and custom database solutions.

Set up Docker

First, install Docker for the developer environment. For information on the supported platforms, read supported platforms (*https://docs.docker.com/install/#supported- platforms*).

section of the Docker Engine Overview. For macOS, we can jump straight to the Docker for Mac install page (*https://docs.docker.com/docker-for-mac/install/*).

If you are working from scratch on an app, the user vapor template for Dockerization is as follows:

```
vapor new my-dockerized-app
```

Follow the prompts to enable or disable relevant features. Your choice of these prompts will affect the generation of the Docker resource files. If you already have an app, copy the templates from a demo dockerized app, as described previously, as a reference point for dockerizing the existing app. We can copy key resources from the template to our app and tweak them as per our app needs. The Vapor App template has two main Docker-specific resources, i.e., the Dockerfile and the Docker-compose file.

The Dockerfile provides information about how to build an image of the Dockerized app. This image contains the Vapor app's executable and all dependencies required to run it. The Dockerfile for the Vapor app has two stages. The first stage builds the app and sets up a holding area for the result. The second stage sets up a secure runtime environment and transfers everything to the holding area, where it will be in the final image. It also sets a default entry point and command, which will run the app in production mode on the default port. We can override this configuration when the image is used.

The Docker Compose file defines how Docker should build multiple services with respect to each other. This file in the template provides the required functionality to deploy the app.

NOTE *If, in the future, you plan to use Kubernetes, the Docker Compose file is not directly relevant. However, Kubernetes manifest files are conceptually similar.*

The Docker Compose file in the Vapor app defines services for running the app, running or reverting migrations, and running the database as per our app's requirements. The exact definitions will vary depending on the database you choose to use:

```
x-shared_environment: &shared_environment
    LOG_LEVEL: ${LOG_LEVEL:-debug}
    DATABASE_HOST: dbHost
    DATABASE_NAME: database
    DATABASE_USERNAME: username
    DATABASE_PASSWORD: password
```

These will be there in multiple services below with **<<: *shared_environment** YAML reference syntax.

The **DATABASE_HOST**, **DATABASE_NAME**, **DATABASE_USERNAME**, and **DATABASE_PASSWORD** variables are hardcoded in the example, but the **LOG_LEVEL** will have a value from the environment running the service.

NOTE *Hard-coding usernames and passwords are not acceptable beyond local development. One way to handle this in production is to store these variables in a secret file, export this file to the environment that is running your deployment, and use the lines shown as follows in the Docker Compose file.*

```
DATABASE_USERNAME: ${DATABASE_USERNAME}
```

Build and Run

Docker knows how to build the app through the Docker Compose file. To build a Docker image for our app, run the following command:

```
cd root directory(containing docker-compose.yml) of the app's project
```

```
docker compose build
```

The app and its dependencies must be built again, irrespective of whether you had previously built them or not on the development machine. When this is done, we will find the app's image while it is running:

```
docker image ls
```

A stack of services can be run from the Docker Compose file, or we can use an orchestration layer like Kubernetes.

The simplest way to run the app is to start it as a standalone container. Docker, using the **depends_on** arrays, makes sure that any dependent services are also started:

```
docker compose up app
```

We will notice that both the **app** and **db** services have started. The **app** is listening on default port **8080** and made accessible on the development machine at **http://localhost:8080**, as defined by the Docker Compose file.

When you see both the database and app running in containers, we can check the logs by running the following command:

```
docker logs <container_id>
```

Production Deployment

As discussed at the start of this section, we will not go into many details about deploying the dockerized app to production as this topic is very large and varies depending on the hosting service, such as AWS, Azure, and so on.

However, the techniques we discussed to run our dockerized app locally on a development machine are mostly transferable to production environments. A server instance that is set up to run the Docker daemon will accept the same commands.

Copy project files to your server, SSH into the server, and run the Docker-compose deploy command to make things run remotely.

IOS APP DEPLOYMENT

Now our server app is deployed for the world, and it is time to deploy our iOS app on the App Store so that users can download our iOS app on their phones.

The first step toward deploying the iOS app is to enroll in the Apple Developer Program (*https://developer.apple.com/programs/enroll/*).

Code Signing

First, we need to create an iOS distribution provisioning profile and distribution certificate in order to distribute our app to beta testers or to users through the App Store.

The easiest way to do this is through Xcode. Open the iOS project in Xcode, click on the project, and navigate to **Signing & Capabilities**, as shown in the following figure. Check **Automatically manage signing**:

FIGURE 10.4 Signing and capabilities.

Click on the **Add Account** button and add your developer account, as shown in the following figure:

FIGURE 10.5 Add account.

Create App Store Connect Record for the App

Create your own App Store Connect organization (*https://developer.apple.com/support/app-store-connect/#//apple_ref/doc/uid/TP40011225-CH25-SW1*). Sign in with the Apple ID, the same ID used to enroll in the Apple Developer Program.

After logging in, you will arrive at the App Store Connect home page, as shown in the following figure:

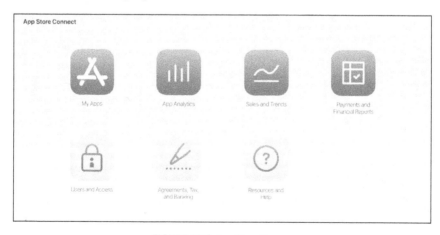

FIGURE 10.6 App Store Connect.

Add New App

In the App Store Connect dashboard, select **My Apps**, then click on the + button in the upper left corner, and then select New App.

Fill in all details, such as platform, app name, default language, bundle ID, SKU, and so on. These information pieces cannot be changed later; therefore, take precautions while entering these details.

The bundle ID must exactly match the bundle identifier in our Xcode project's **Info. plist** file. **SKU** is an abbreviation for a stock-keeping unit. SKU must be a unique ID for our app in the Apple system that is not visible to users. We can use letters, numbers, hyphens, periods, and underscores, but we cannot start with a hyphen, period, or underscore. Should create a value that is meaningful to your organization.

Archive and Upload the App

Before we can submit our app for review through App Store Connect, we first need to upload the build through Xcode. In Xcode, select Generic iOS Device as the deployment target, as shown in the following figure:

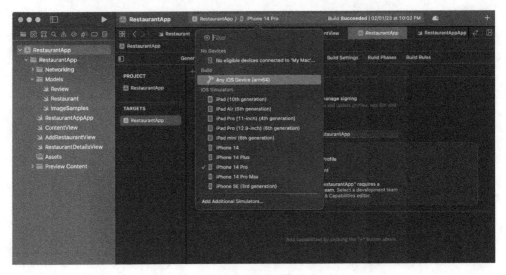

FIGURE 10.7 iOS build.

Choose **Product** | **Archive** as shown in the following figure:

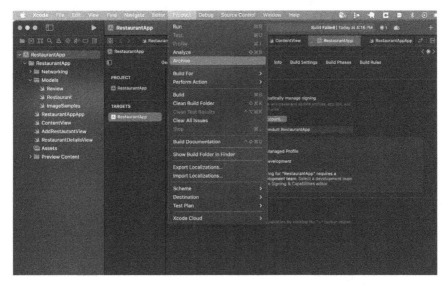

FIGURE 10.8 Archive.

This will launch Xcode Organizer, which will display the list of archives you have created in the past as well. Choose the current one and click on **Upload to App Store** in the right panel. Select your credentials, click **Choose**, and follow the screens to finally upload the build. After completing the upload, a success message will appear, as shown in the following figure:

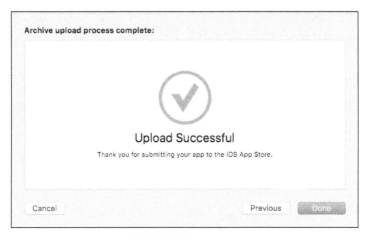

FIGURE 10.9 Upload archive.

Configure the App's Metadata in App Store Connect

Select the **App   Store** tab in App Store Connect, and on the **App Information** page, you can add metadata such as languages, categories, and your app's Privacy Policy URL, as shown in the following figure:

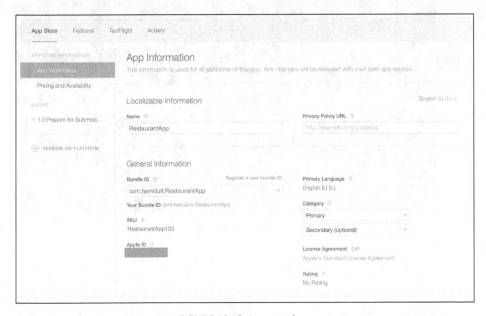

FIGURE 10.10 App metadata.

You can set pricing as free or at your selected price on the **Pricing and Availability** page after clicking **Pricing and Availability** just below the **App Store** tab in the left pane.

In the **Features** tab under the **App Store**, we can add configurations like Game Center and in-app purchases.

At this stage, our app has the status **Prepare for Submission** and is marked with a yellow dot in the left pane under **App Store**, as shown in the following figure:

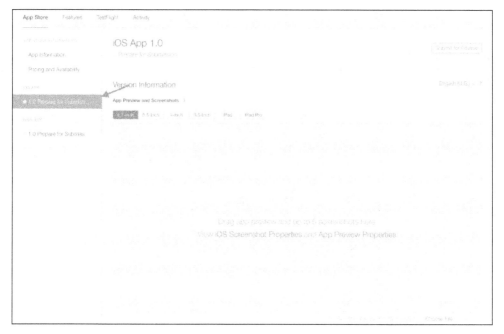

FIGURE 10.11 Prepare for submission.

Select the build we want to configure and add the information for the product page.

Upload the app's screenshots (JPEG or PNG). Scroll down and enter the app's description, keywords, support, and marketing URLs. In the **General App Information** section, add the app's icon, version number, copyright, and contact information as per standards. Click on **Edit** next to **Rating** and select the applicable options for the app. In the top-right corner, click **Save**. We are almost ready to submit the app for review.

Submit App for Review

Scroll to the **Build** section in your app's App Store Connect, as shown in the following figure:

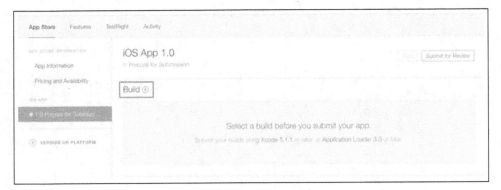

FIGURE 10.12 Build section.

Click on the **"Select a build before you submit your app"** link. Choose the build that we uploaded through Xcode. Click the **Done** button in the bottom right corner, then click the **Save** button in the top right corner. Finally, **Submit for Review**.

Select **Activity** in the top horizontal menu, then **App Store Versions** in the left-hand panel to check on the status of the app, as shown in the following figure:

FIGURE 10.13 App status.

In most cases, it takes about one to three days for approval. In case the app is rejected, you have to make the necessary fixes, as mentioned in the review comments, and resubmit again. If your app is approved, congratulations!

You can now download your app from the App Store and view downloads, sales, ratings, and so on in the App Store Connect.

CONCLUSION

With this chapter, we can conclude our journey through this book, and you are ready to explore the vast space related to swift full-stack development. In this chapter, we discussed various deployment techniques relating to the deployment of the Vapor app and iOS app. With this, we have completed our journey from inception to the deployment of our full-stack project. However, this is not all; this space is vast, and there is a lot more to learn beyond these chapters.

INDEX

A

Apple Push Notification Service (APNS), 211–216
Asynchronous programming, 76
AsyncHTTPClient, 15
Auto Layout with storyboards
  add new constraints menu, 124–125
  align menu, 125–126
  constraint warning, 127–128
  Hello world project
    add constraints, 132
    add new label, 131
    constraints in in layout mode, 135
    constraints in portrait mode, 135
    Fix Misplacement button, 129
    simulator result, 130
    T-Bars without conflicts, 130
    Vertical Spacing and Leading constraints, 133
  T-Bars, 127

C

Core Data
  to an existing project, 152–153
  Class Definition, 158–159
  Codegen section, 157–158
  CRUD operations
    entities, 154–155
    relationships, 154–156
  migration
    heavyweight migration, 161
    lightweight migration, 161–164
  in new project, 151
  stack, 159
  stack, 150
Create, Read, Update, and Delete operations (CRUD), 107–110

F

Fluent, 104–107
Full-stack, 5

APNs, 211–216
middleware, 206–209
mobile app developer, 5
security
    basic authentication, 217–218
    Bearer authentication, 219–220
    composition, 220–222
    JWT, 224–226
    keychain, 226–229
    session-based authentication, 222–224
WebSockets
    close method, 211
    sending and receiving messages, 211
Full-stack developer, 2
Full-stack development
    advantages of, 10–11
    description, 2
    history of, 4
    problems with, 7–9
Full-stack implementation
    project outline, 168
    Restaurant-Server app
        config and routes, 180–183
        controllers, 177–180
        create, 171
        migrations, 175–177
        models, 172–175
    setup remote database, 168–170

H
Hello World project
    iOS
        Project configuration, 30
        project directory, 30
        project structure, 31
        project template, 29
        UI design, 35

UI object library, 34
ViewController Scene, 32–33
Xcode Project, 27–28
Vapor toolbox, installation of
    build and run, 22–24
    folder structure, 24–26

I
iOS app deployment
    App metadata, 244
    App Store Connect, 241
    archive and upload, 242–243
    select New App, 242
    signing & capabilities, 240–241
    submit app for review, 245–246

J
JSON, 63–72

L
Leaf templates, 87–94
Logging, 77
    SwiftLog, 78

M
Migrations, 110–112
Minimum viable product (MVP), 3, 5–6
    features, 6
Model-view-controller (MVC), 55–63

N
Network requests, 164–165

P
PostgreSQL
    installation and setting up, 97–103
    non-relational databases, 96
    relational databases, 96

Postico, 112–116
Protocol support, 165

R
`RestaurantApp`
  models, 185–187
  networking
    delete function, 188
    getAllRestaurants() function, 189
    get reviews function, 191
    HTTP client, 188
    save restaurant function, 190
    saveReview function, 191–192
  test run, 201–203
  user interface, 192–200
Routes, 42–43
Run Xcode project, 35–39

S
Soto, 16–17
Swift
  packages, 14
  for server applications, 11
  Vapor, 11–12
Swift AWS Lambda Runtime, 16
SwiftNIO, 14–15
Swift Package Manager (SPM), 14, 26–27
SwiftUI
  canvas and preview feature, 136
  stacks, 144–148
  text properties, 137–140
  working with images, 140–144

T
`todo` model
  create, 116
  save

browser error, 118
`GET` request, 120
Postgres server, 118
`POST` request, 119
`routes.swift`, 117
`TodoController` class, 117

V
Vapor
  environment, 79–80
  errors
    `AbortError`, 80–82
    `DebuggableError`, 83–84
  Leaf templates, 87–94
  router methods
    basic routes, 43–44
    catch-all route, 50–52
    multiple route parameters, 49
    nested routes, 44–46
    parameterized routes, 48
    query strings, 52–53
    route groups, 53–54
    route parameters, 47–48
    with two parameters, 50
  stack traces, 85–87
Vapor app deployment
  Docker
    benefits, 237
    build and run, 239
    production, 239–240
    set up, 237–238
  Heroku, 232–236
Vapor toolbox, installation of, 21

X
Xcode, installation of, 20–21

www.ingramcontent.com/pod-product-compliance
Lightning Source LLC
LaVergne TN
LVHW062310060326
832902LV00013B/2136